THE
HUEY
AND
HUEY COBRA

This book is dedicated to the thousands of men and women who have flown and are still flying the Hueys and HueyCobras in war, in commercial service, and on humanitarian missions.

THE
HUEY
AND
HUEY COBRA

BILL SIURU

TAB BOOKS Inc.
Blue Ridge Summit, PA 17214

FIRST EDITION

FIRST PRINTING

Copyright © 1987 by TAB BOOKS Inc.

Printed in the United States of America

Library of Congress Cataloging in Publication Data

Siuru, William D.
    The Huey and HueyCobra.

    Includes index.
    1. Huey Cobra (Helicopter) I. Title.
UG1233.S58 1987   623.7'6047   86-28840
ISBN 0-8306-8393-3 (pbk.)

Questions regarding the content of this book
should be addressed to:

    Reader Inquiry Branch
    Editorial Department
    TAB BOOKS Inc.
    P.O. Box 40
    Blue Ridge Summit, PA 17214

Cover photograph courtesy of Bell Helicopters Textron.

Contents

Acknowledgments

This book could not have been written without the help of many individuals who supplied illustrations and photographs, many of which have never been published before. Special thanks go to Richard Tipton, Public Affairs at Bell Helicopters Textron, for supplying just the right photography when needed.

Others who made this book possible include:

Agusta S.P.A., especially, Bianca Corbella.
Avco Lycoming.
Bell Aerospace Textron, especially, Robert N. Sherwood.
Canadian Forces.
Emerson Electric Company.
General Electric, Aircraft Business Group, especially, Virginia M. Wilke.
General Electric, Armament and Electrical Systems Department, especially, C. F. Bushey.
Hughes Aircraft Corporation.
Hughes Helicopters.
Israeli Embassy, Washington, D.C.
Kaman Corporation, especially, Dana Baltauskas.
Lockheed California Company.
McDonnell Douglas Helicopters.
National Safety Council of Australia.

Patton Museum of Cavalry and Armor, especially, David A. Holt.

Rockwell International

Sikorsky Aircraft Company.

U.S. Air Force, 1776th Air Base Wing (MAC), especially, Jeffrey S. Legeer.

U.S. Air Force, 56th Tactical Training Wing (TAC), especially, Lieutenant Susan E. Declercq.

U.S. Air Force in Europe, especially, Lt. Colonel William H. Johnson.

U.S. Army Aviation Museum, especially, James G. Craig and Thomas J. Sabiston.

U.S. Army Europe and Seventh Army, especially, Guenther Jeschke.

U.S. Army Aviation Logistics School, especially, Otis L. Haislip.

U.S. Army Transportation Center, especially, Ruth E. Shepard.

U.S. Customs Service, especially, Dennis H. Murphy.

U.S. Marine Corps, Headquarters, especially, Lt. Colonel J. M. Shotwell.

U.S. Navy Photographic Services.

Introduction

Throughout aviation there have been numerous aircraft that can be considered "classics." The P-51 Mustang, the Spitfire, the DC-3, the Lockheed Constellation, the Beech Staggerwing, and the Piper Cub immediately come to mind, and many more can be included in the classic status. When it comes to helicopters—which are more utilitarian in both looks and purpose—there is really only one that the aviation enthusiast would probably consider a classic.

The Bell Huey—and its variants—has been produced by the thousands for over three decades, and it is still in production. In that time, it has seen service in virtually every war that has been waged anywhere in the world. Both commercial and military versions are as familiar to people around the free world as the Volkswagen. The Huey has been built on three continents and total production has exceeded the 25,000 mark, a claim that only a handful of aircraft in all of aviation history can make. Hueys will be flying well into the twenty-first century. The list of Huey derivatives and variants is extremely long, with the basic designs adapted to do a multitude of jobs.

The Huey made possible the military concepts of air mobility and the helicopter gunship. The HueyCobra pioneered the attack helicopter, the rotary-wing version of the fighter aircraft. Helicopters in general—and the Huey and HueyCobra specifically—added a third dimension to a ground army's battlefield: the air. The Huey was the first helicopter to be used as a combat aircraft by the U.S.

Army, seeing extensive action in Southeast Asia. Not only did the Huey and HueyCobra perform in an heroic manner, they also taught the military important lessons about helicopter warfare and provided much experience in helicopter tactics that will become even more useful in the future. The Huey is the only aircraft that is used extensively by all four of our military services: the Army, Navy, Air Force, and Marines.

The Huey also played a significant role in advancing helicopter technology. The use of a gas turbine engine in the Huey transformed the helicopter from a rather fragile, maintenance-intensive aircraft to a machine that could be used just about anywhere with a minimum of support. It also significantly boosted the helicopter's performance. The Huey's history contains a long list of firsts and record-setting flights. Much of the technology pioneered in the Huey and HueyCobra would be used later in the newest utility and attack helicopters.

This book attempts to tell the complete story by covering all the models of the Huey and HueyCobra, whether produced by the hundreds or as a single copy. By looking at each of the models, the evolution of the world's most popular helicopter can be traced over a period that spans three decades. The book is oriented both to the person who wants to learn more about the fascinating story of the helicopter as well as those aviation buffs who want "all the details." The story of the Huey and HueyCobra is a visual story and thus the multitude of photographs included in this book in most cases tell the story far better than words ever can.

Chapter 1

The Huey's Ancestors

Like so many other inventions, the helicopter was developed to meet the urgencies of war. Oh yes, ever since men began to dream about flying, they thought about craft that could take off and land without large areas of real estate. However, for years the technology was not available to build a helicopter that worked. Many tried, but most failed in attempts to build a vertical-lift craft. It was the aviation genius Igor Sikorsky who finally achieved success; he was able to get his helicopter design into service near the end of World War II. (Incidentally, Sikorsky had experimented with helicopters in the early 1900s before he gave up in frustration and went on to other things, such as the world's first production four-engined airplane and the famous Sikorsky flying boats, which pioneered transoceanic air travel.) Sikorsky envisioned the helicopter as an aircraft primarily for rescue and lifesaving work. Indeed, this would be the first use for his pioneer R-4 helicopters. But before he died at the age of 83, he would see his invention turned into a potent instrument of war.

The helicopter was introduced as World War II was winding down, so the few dozen Sikorsky R-4s produced were used either for experiments or for special rescue operations. For instance, most of the choppers bought by the U.S. Navy went to the Coast Guard for rescue work. In 1943, Admiral Ernest King, the Navy's chief, had given the U.S. Coast Guard the responsibility for using the

Igor Sikorsky personally piloted the VS-300 on its maiden flight on September 14, 1939. (courtesy Sikorsky Aircraft)

helicopter at sea. Military and naval leaders did not yet see the helicopter as an aircraft for combat.

While several units claim the honor of being the first to use a chopper to perform a rescue behind enemy lines, the honor should go to the Army's First Commando Group. The Group was fighting the Japanese in Burma alongside General Wingate's Raiders. In April 1944, a light liason airplane carrying an American pilot and three British infantrymen, two wounded and one sick with malaria, crashed behind enemy lines in the inaccessible Burmese jungle. Lt.

The Sikorsky R-4 was developed in time to see limited duty during World War II. (courtesy USAF)

The Bell XP-59A was America's first jet aircraft. (courtesy Bell Aerospace Textron)

Carter Harmon flew his Sikorsky R-4C to rescue the men, one by one, from a tiny rice paddy.

In the last days of World War II, other R-4s were called in to perform rescues where only a craft that could hover and fly vertically to make a pinpoint landing could do the job. The helicopter had gained its place in the military inventory, even though it was still considered a noncombatant.

Immediately after the war many companies large and small became interested in helicopters. One of them was Bell Aircraft, already well established in the fixed-wing aircraft business, having

The Bell Model 47 was an extremely popular helicopter. The Army gave it the family designation H-13 and the name "Sioux." (courtesy U.S. Army Aviation Museum)

The stabilizer bar, which has been a characteristic part of Bell Helicopter designs for many years. (courtesy Bell Helicopters Textron)

developed such famous aircraft as the XP-59A, America's first jet-powered aircraft. Bell Aircraft was also a pioneer in helicopters, its Model 30 having first flown on July 29, 1943. One of the features of the Model 30 was a stabilizer bar, which would be found on Bell-produced helicopters (including the Hueys) for many years. This stabilizer bar was a short bar set perpendicular to the main rotor blades and had streamlined counterweights at each end.

In 1946, Bell brought out its Model 47 helicopter, the first helicopter to be granted a commercial license by the Federal Aviation Administration (at that time, the CAA). In 1951, Bell Aircraft established a helicopter division headed by Lawrence Bell. The Model 47, produced for an amazing 27 years, was probably the most popular helicopter ever produced before the Huey. The military version, the OH-13, was used for jobs ranging from medical evacuation and reconnaissance to the training of fledgling helicopter pilots. The Sioux, as the OH-13 was called by the Army, saw extensive service in the Korean conflict. Bell gained valuable experience with its civilian and military versions of the Model 47—experience that would be applied to the Hueys it would be designing and building in the next few years. Indeed, Lawrence Bell even visited the battle zone in Korea to witness his helicopters in action.

While on the subject of Korea, we cannot neglect mentioning

the contributions made by rotary-wing craft during these hostilities. In Korea, the helicopter received its baptism of fire and proved itself in combat. The military gained valuable experience and important information about the capabilities it wanted in the next generation of military choppers.

The helicopter was used extensively in Korea for rescuing downed pilots, often in the midst of enemy gunfire. The exploits of these courageous rescue crews have been captured in several stories, books, and movies, including James A. Michener's *The*

Lawrence "Larry" Bell, a pioneer and visionary in Helicopters. (courtesy Bell Helicopters Textron)

Many a pilot in the Korean War was rescued by an H-19 like this one. (courtesy USAF)

Bridges at Toko-Ri. The helicopter proved itself in the medical evacuation role. It was able to pick up the wounded soldier—often right on the battlefield where he had fallen—and fly him directly to a field hospital. This feat, before the advent of the helicopter,

Right from the start of the Korean War, helicopters like this Marine Corps HO3S-1 were used in support of ground troops. (courtesy Sikorsky Aircraft)

Helicopters such as these USAF H-5s played a tremendous role in dramatically reducing combat casualties in Korea. (courtesy USAF)

might have taken days; it could now be done in a matter of hours. During its first three months of operation, the Army's original Mobile Army Surgical Hospital (the *M*A*S*H* of television fame) was able to transport nearly 2000 wounded GIs using only 11 choppers. And this was done often carrying only one wounded troop at a time while under enemy ground fire. The helicopter saved many lives and substantially reduced the casualty rate in Korea.

The U.S. Marine Corps was the first to exploit the chopper to deliver fully equipped troops onto the battlefield ready to fight. In the fall of 1951, the Marines used their new HRS helicopter (Sikorsky CH-19) to deploy hundreds of Leathernecks into combat during *Operation Summit*; this was followed by *Operation Bumblebee*, where a 950-man battalion was transported to meet the enemy. The helicopter was found to be ideal for the vertical assault job, a mission that would be refined by both the Marines and Army after the Korean War. This mission would be the driving force in the design of the Huey and proved so important in Vietnam. (Incidentally, the Marines liked to carry Korean soldiers because they were smaller and more of them could fit into the choppers.)

The helicopter found many other jobs to its liking during Korea. For instance, choppers were used as scouts for mine sweepers. From their vantage point in the sky, it was easier to see floating mines in the water than from surface ships. For a while, the chopper crews fired rifles at the mines to explode them—that is, until one of them exploded and touched off several other mines, nearly knocking the chopper out of the sky. That ended this dangerous practice.

One of the more daring chopper escapades was a secret mission to bring back a downed Russian MiG fighter from beyond the North Korean frontier. The intelligence experts wanted a better look at the fighter our pilots were up against. An H-19 was used to transport a dismantling crew to the crash site. The MiG was taken apart and loaded on the H-19 in less than an hour. It was then hauled back with portions of it sticking out in the wind. Upon landing, the MiG was loaded on another airplane for the journey to the U.S., where it was analyzed in great detail.

The helicopter was now a proven military weapon. However, the Army had some definite ideas on what it wanted in a new helicopter. The Huey would be the aircraft to fulfill the Army's needs—and indeed, the needs of military and commercial users around the world.

Chapter 2

The Huey Is Born

In February 1954, the Army announced the design competition for a new helicopter that eventually would be the Huey. The Army wanted a helicopter that could carry a 800-pound payload on a 200-nautical mile (227-mile) round trip with a 100-knot (114-mph) cruising speed. The new craft was intended for transporting troops, supplies, and equipment, as well as for rushing wounded soldiers from the battlefield to a hospital. The Army asked for a helicopter that could easily be carried in a cargo transport such as the USAF's C-124s and C-130s, so that it could be used to support the Army's global mission.

Ease of maintenance right in the field was important to the Army, for while the helicopter had proven itself in battle during Korea, it was notorious for its frequency of breakdowns. Many hours of maintenance were often required to keep a chopper in the air for an hour or so. It should be noted that even the simplest helicopter is a complex piece of machinery—much more complex than a comparable fixed-wing airplane. Add to this the fact that a helicopter's flight can be described as a "series of coordinated vibrations" and you can see why maintenance and reliability can be such a headache.

The Gas Turbine Engine

One thing that would make the new Army's new utility helicop-

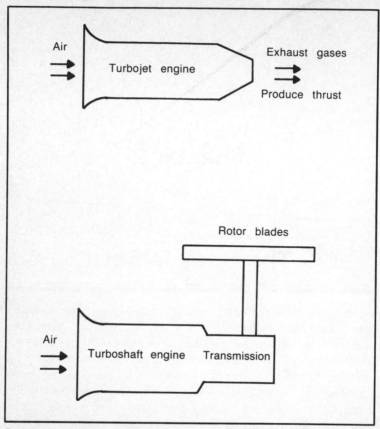

Both the turbojet and turboshaft engines are gas turbine powerplants. While the turbojet provides propulsion through its exhaust gases, the turboshaft uses these gases to drive a turbine, which in turn provides shaft power. In the case of a helicopter, the output shaft drives the rotor through a transmission.

ter more reliable and easier to maintain would be its gas turbine engine. In the mid-1950s, jet engines were powering most of the world's bombers and fighters; jet airliners, such as the Boeing 707, were just over the horizon. Development of the turboshaft engine, an offshoot of the pure jet engine, had progressed to the point where it was a logical choice for use in a helicopter. Up until the Huey, piston engines were used to power U.S. Army helicopters.

In 1951, the Kaman K-225 was the first helicopter to be powered by a gas turbine engine. It used a turbine made by Boeing. Three years later, another Kaman helicopter, the HTK-1, was powered by twin Boeing gas turbines, each producing 190 horsepower. Both engines together weighed the same as the single

The Kaman K-225 was the world's first helicopter to be powered by a gas turbine engine. It flew in 1951, and was almost as rudimentary as Sikorsky's first helicopter, the VS300. (courtesy Kaman Corporation)

240-horsepower piston engine that normally powered the HTK-1, but the jets provided over 50 percent more power, revealing the potential advantage of turbine-powered helicopters. The French-made SNCA-S.E. 3130 Alouette II, which first flew in 1955, was

The helicopter that started the Huey legacy, the XH-40. (courtesy Bell Helicopters Textron)

The workings of the Lycoming turboshaft engine used in the Hueys. At left is the transmission that drives the rotor. Air enters the engine from the right side. (courtesy Avco Lycoming)

the first turbine-powered helicopter to go into quantity production and was continued in production until 1975.

Both the turbojet and turboshaft engines are gas turbines, the principal difference being that in the turboshaft engine, the high-velocity gases are used to drive a power turbine which in turn drives the rotor shaft through a transmission, thus the name *turboshaft*. In a pure-jet engine, the exhaust gases provide the thrust to propel the aircraft through the air.

The XH-40 had a somewhat shorter fuselage than the HU-1A, the first Huey that went into production.

One of the three XH-40 prototypes shares a place of honor at the U.S. Army Aviation Museum at Fort Rucker, Alabama. (courtesy U.S. Army Aviation Museum)

Turboshaft engines are less complex and have fewer parts than piston engines. Not only is the turbine simpler, it is lighter. For example, the 1275-horsepower engine found in a Sikorsky H-19 weighed on the order of 3500 pounds. Contrast this to the 1100-horsepower turbine used in later models of the Huey, weighed around only a ton. This weight savings can be directly translated into payload. Besides these advantages, the turbine is easier to start and does not require time to warm up before flight. Also, a gas turbine engine is smaller and can be mounted on top of the helicopter, allowing more interior cargo room. However, a gas turbine engine does guzzle more fuel, the fuel being JP-4 or kerosene versus high-octane aviation gasoline.

Bell can be credited with pioneering the application of turboshaft technology with its first use of a gas turbine engine in an Army helicopter. However, development of the actual engine, designated the XT53, was done by Avco Lycoming, which had started work on the engine under U.S. government sponsorship in 1952.

HX-40 and YH-40

From some 20 companies that entered the competition for a new utility helicopter, Bell Helicopter was picked as the winner.

Bell Helicopter was an offshoot of the Bell Aircraft Corporation, which had been established in 1951 to build helicopters such as the Model 47 and H-13. By June 1955, Bell was awarded a contract to build three prototype XH-40s, the original designation for the Huey. Bell called it the Model 204. With great speed and efficiency at its Ft. Worth, Texas, facility, Bell was ready with the first XH-40 in just over a year.

The maiden flight of the XH-40 was made in October 1956, with veteran Bell test pilot Floyd Carlson at the controls. This was a mere 16 months after the project had officially begun. As this chopper took off there was the typical "wop-wop" sound, but added to this familiar noise was a new sound, one that would become synonymous with military helicopters—the whine of a turbine engine. It is quite appropriate that Floyd Carlson would be at the controls on this first flight of the Huey, for he had piloted Bell's first helicopter, the Model 30, in 1943. Unfortunately, Larry Bell was not able to witness this historic flight, for he had died only two days earlier, on October 20, 1956.

The XH-40 prototypes had the characteristic Huey appearance—which would become so familiar in the next couple of decades—even though the design would be greatly modified and improved through the years. The XH-40's single turboshaft engine produced 700 horsepower. With this amount of power, the XH-40

The YH-40 was closer in design to the HU-1A that actually went into production. (courtesy Bell Helicopters Textron)

The HU-1A, later the UH-1A, was the first Huey to see service with the U.S. Army. Comparing it with photos of the XH-40, you will see the main changes, including a revised rotor shaft fairing. (courtesy Bell Helicopters Textron)

could lift a total weight of just under 5800 pounds. Of this weight, about 2200 pounds was in crew, passengers, and useful payload. Normal accommodations were for four passengers or two litter patients and two attendants. Incidentally, the XH-40 program was initiated by the U.S. Army Medical Corps. Among the XH-40's key features were the large sliding doors on either side of the passenger cabin and the knee-high floor, which made loading and unloading quite easy. The XH-40 had a top speed of 121 knots (138 mph) and could cruise along at 110 knots (125 mph). Maximum range was over 254 nautical miles (290 miles).

Shortly after the first flight of the XH-40, the Army placed an order for six YH-40s. The YH-40 had a 12-inch long fuselage to give more room for stretchers. There was space for eight troops or four stretchers plus a pilot and copilot. Gone was the domelike fairing at the base of the rotor shaft. The YH-40s also has 4 additional inches of ground clearance and some modifications to the controls. The gas turbine engine now produced 770 horsepower.

The nine Hueys would be tested extensively by both Army test pilots and by actual Army units in the field. They were tested in conditions from the extremely cold temperatures of Alaska to the desert heat of Edwards AFB, California, for this was just a sampling of the environments that the Huey would have to operate in. In comparison to many other new aircraft projects—and the XH-40 was a *revolutionarily* new aircraft—the program went very smoothly, with very few technical or financial problems. The three XH-40s and six YH-40s, complete with spares, cost the Army just under 30 million dollars.

HU-1A or UH-1A

While testing was still underway in 1958, the production of Hueys was started, with the first one leaving the Bell factory in September 1958. These first production models were designated as HU-1As, a designation that would be contracted into the unofficial name "Huey." The official name was Iroquis, in line with the Army's policy of naming helicopters after Indian tribes. The HU-1A nomenclature was changed later to UH-1A as the result of a change in the way the U.S. military designated its aircraft. In each case, the H stood for helicopter and the U for utility. Eventually the Huey title became part of the aircraft design when Bell started putting the words "Bell" and "Huey" on the left and right rudder pedals respectively.

The first HU-1 was shipped to Alaska for cold weather testing. Other HU-1s were tested with a variety of weapons mounted on them. These included French-made Nord SS11 and Nord AGM-22A wire-guided missiles. In a wire-guided missile, the missile is controlled in flight using wires that are unfurled from the rear of the missile as the weapon travels from the helicopter to the target. Electrical signals are sent along the wire to the missile's control surfaces. Other weapons tested included four Emerson M73 7.62mm machine guns, a General Electric grenade launcher, and 70mm rockets. While designed for utility and medical evacuation missions, the Army was already interested in the Huey as a weapons platform.

The HU-1A or UH-1A was essentially the same as the YH-40 except that it was powered with an 860-horsepower Lycoming T53-L-1A engine giving a maximum speed of 130 knots (148 mph), a gross weight of 8500 pounds, and a range of 335 nautical miles (382 miles).

In all, 182 Bell Model 204s were made. These included the UH-1As plus other variants, including 14 fitted with instrument flying equipment and dual controls. The latter were designated TH-1As and were used for pilot training at Fort Rucker, Alabama, the home of Army aviation. The early UH-1As were assigned to light aviation units in Europe and Korea. The first A model Hueys were shipped to Vietnam and used by the 57th Medical Detachment for air ambulance service. As the name of the unit implies, these UH-1As were used for medical evacuation, or medevac as it more commonly came to be known. (They were also later called "dust-off" missions in the slang of the troops in Vietnam.)

Chapter 3

The Huey and Airmobility

Vietnam has been called the helicopter war, for not only were choppers used by the thousands, but the doctrine and tactics of the war were shaped around the capabilities of the helicopter. In Vietnam there were no fixed battlefields and the Vietnamese landscape with its swamps and rice paddies was on obstacle to conventional troop movement on the ground. While helicopters performed what the chopper pilots call "ash and trash missions," meaning everything from medevac to carrying supplies, the helicopter became an assault transport, armed gunship, and, finally, an attack aircraft. The development of these helicopters of war centered around the Bell Model 204 family of helicopters and its descendents.

Airmobility

While the Hueys were being developed, the U.S. Army was also refining the concept of *airmobility*, a concept that would fully capitalize on the capabilities of the Huey. In simple terms, airmobility means using aircraft as an integral part of the ground commander's inventory of weapons. Aircraft, both fixed- and rotary-wing, give the ground commander a platform in the sky for gathering intelligence data, providing command and control over ground operations, and extending his firepower. Most importantly, airmobility adds a new dimension of mobility for ground forces; troops can be rapidly deployed where and when they are needed.

The UH-1A was the first Huey to see action in Vietnam, arriving there in late 1961. (courtesy U.S. Army)

While it appears that the U.S. Air Force and Navy seem best able to supply air support, the key to airmobility is the fact that the aircraft are assigned to and commanded by an Army commander who uses them just as he uses his infantry, armor, and artillery resources. He is in the best position to know how organic airpower can be used most effectively.

The airmobility concept is an extension of airborne deployment, in which forces can be parachuted into battle quickly and with an element of surprise. In many ways it is quite similar; in others it is quite different. The similarity lies in the fact that both involve movement of troops quickly by air to where they are needed. For airborne troops, this means by specially equipped USAF cargo aircraft. In airmobility, troop movement is by helicopters. The differences come from the characteristics of fixed-wing transports versus helicopter troop carriers. USAF transports can carry large numbers of troops great distances. Therefore, units can be stationed in the United States and quite feasibly be dropped on any trouble spot in the world—and they can be dropped in huge numbers.

The helicopter is a short-range transport that carries a rather limited payload. Therefore, it is best used as a Jeep or truck carrying a limited number of men around the battlefield as they are needed. The helicopter has a trait not found in the normal transports: It can be used to *withdraw* troops when the battle is over or things get too hot. While the helicopter was used for troop transport on a limited basis in Korea, mainly by the Marines, the refinement of the airmobility concept would have to wait until the 1960s and the Vietnam war. The Huey would play a key role in this refinement.

Even though the airmobility concept did not come into its own until the war in Vietnam, the Army was planning for it even as far back as the early 1950s, when the term "airmobility" first appeared. Incidentally, the British had used rudimentary forms of airmobility during its operations in Malaya, as did the French in Algeria. In the early 1960s the Army Tactical Mobility Requirements Board was established with General Hamilton Howze as President. The Howze Board, as it was popularly called, wrote the book on airmobility doctrine.

Before we go on, a few terms should be defined for clarity as to the types of helicopters used in Vietnam. The *assault transport* is a chopper whose main purpose is to deliver fully equipped troops on the battlefield ready to fight. It can also withdraw them when required. The *armed helicopter* is a helicopter that carries armament

This is what airmobility is all about—combat-equipped troops disembarking from Huey "slick." (courtesy U.S. Army)

for helicopter escort and direct fire support missions. These are standard utility and cargo helicopters that were converted to gunships by adding on armament packages. (In Vietnam, virtually every Army, Navy, Air Force, or Marine Corps helicopter was armed in some way or other, usually by makeshift, in-the-field addition of ordnance; however, the term *armed helicopter* is reserved here for those helicopters with specifically designed armament packages.) Finally, there is the *attack helicopter*, which is designed from the ground up with integral weapons for the single purpose of providing optimum escort, direct fire, and anti-armor support. It is the rotary-wing equivalent of the fixed-wing close air support fighter.

The Army started quite early with armed helicopters. In the early 1950s, helicopters were fitted with weapons to demonstrate the firepower of the helicopter. First it was merely a machine gun strapped to an H-13 whirlybird. Then there was the Army's Aerial Combat Reconnaissance Platoon with a handful of helicopters armed with a variety of improvised weapons, mostly scrounged from the scrap heap. Probably one of the more potent pre-Huey gunships was a Sikorsky H-34 chopper that had been fitted with 40 2.75-inch rockets, two five-inch high velocity aircraft rockets (HVAR), three .50-caliber machine guns, six .30-caliber machine guns, and two 20mm cannons. This flying arsenal (called, appropriately, Project AMMO) could have proven a very potent weapon

The UH-1B was the first Huey to be built in massive quantities. (courtesy Bell Helicopters Textron)

When unarmed, the Huey (here, a UH-1B) was called a "slick." (courtesy Bell Helicopters Textron)

system had it gone into production. As mentioned previously, various ordnance was tested on the earliest models of the HU-1.

The Army also tried a unique helicopter gun platform. An H-34 was fitted with 20 4.5-inch rockets. But instead of firing from the air, the helicopter would land and the whole chopper would be swiveled and aimed just like a cannon. After the rockets were fired, the helicopter would take off and fly home to reload.

The Huey, with its wide doors and low floor, was designed for ease of loading and unloading. (courtesy U.S. Army)

Ground crews in Vietnam could reload and refuel Hueys in a matter of minutes. (courtesy U.S. Army)

The Hueys Come to Vietnam

Right from the start, helicopters played a major role in our involvement in Vietnam. Two Army helicopter companies arrived in Nam in December 1961 and were quickly put to work transporting thousands of Vietnamese troops into battle against the Viet

Huey gunship crews take a brief break before going back into action. (courtesy U.S. Army)

This Huey is engaged in a rescue attempt while troops on the ground are in contact with the enemy. (courtesy U.S. Army)

Cong. While originally unarmed, the H-21 crews hastily armed their craft when fired upon by the Viet Cong. These early airmobile helicopters were usually equipped with a .30-caliber Browning or M60 machine gun or two located in the door.

The first armed Hueys, 15 UH-1As, arrived in Vietnam in the fall of 1962. These gunships were usually equipped with .30-caliber machine guns mounted on their sides near the nose, pods for 16 2.75-inch rockets, and machine guns for two door gunners. The weaponry was added when the UH-1As got to Southeast Asia. The first Huey gunships were assigned the job of providing protective fire for the CH-21 Shawnee assault transport helicopters. Because this was an experiment, the first armed UH-1As were carefully watched by the Army Concept Team in Vietnam. The Army learned many lessons from these early experiments, lessons that would be used when airmobility operations would be expanded in future years. By the spring of 1963, the UH-1As were also providing armed escort for Marine Corps HU-34 assault transports.

Based on the success of the UH-1A, the UH-1B gunship was born. The UH-1B was the first Huey to come "factory equipped" as a gunship and the first to be produced in sizable quantities, some 991 being made between 1960 and 1964. From its external appearance it is hard to tell a UH-1B from an A model. The main differences is the 960-horsepower T-53-L-5 engine and, later, the 1100-horsepower T53-L-9 or -11 engine. The 1100-horsepower engine boosted the Huey's maximum gross weight by 1300 pounds, its load-carrying ability by 1500 pounds, and its speed by up to about 25 knots (29 mph). In the troop-carrying configuration it could carry eight passengers or three litters for medevac.

In the fall of 1962, 11 UH-1Bs made their appearance in Vietnam. Armament on the initial UH-1Bs included an Emerson turret housing four M60 machine guns just aft of each of the cargo doors. The guns could be operated by the pilot, copilot, or gunner. The turrets had racks for rocket pods and launchers either on top or bottom. This factory armament was often augmented in the field by a variety of guns located within the cabin and operated by the door gunner or crew chief.

As more UH-1Bs came in-country, they were used as troop transports to replace the aging Shawnees. These Hueys, referred to generically as "slicks," had a minimum of armament, usually door-mounted M60 machine guns.

The Eagle Flights of the early war years demonstrate how the Hueys were employed. A typical Eagle Flight consisted of 14 Hueys. One of the armed gunship helicopters would serve as an airborne command post. Five more of the armed Hueys would provide escort and covering fire for the seven slicks carrying troops. The 14th helicopter would be ready to provide medical evacuation. The Eagle Flight would normally stand alert awaiting orders either on the ground or in the air. Once scrambled, the armed gunships would proceed to the landing site and engage the enemy, making a few passes while firing weapons. Once the landing site was secure, the troop ships would land and discharge their passengers. Meanwhile, the armed gunships would continue to sup-

During the Vietnam conflict, not all Army Hueys were in action in the war. This Huey was one of three that were the first helicopters to land at the South Pole in February 1963. (courtesy U.S. Army)

The Army uses the Huey extensively as a flying crane for delivering supplies. (courtesy U.S. Army)

press enemy firepower to protect the choppers and men on the ground. After only a few minutes to unload, the slicks would take off for home under the protective wing of the gunships.

Unfortunately, when the UH-1B carried its full load of armament, ammunition, and crew, the gunship was loaded to its maxi-

Production of Hueys reached its peak at Bell Helicopter's Fort Worth facilities in the mid 1960s during the height of the Vietnamese War. (courtesy Bell Helicopters Textron)

A close-up shot of the launchers for the 2.75-inch Folding Fin Aerial Rockets. (courtesy U.S. Army)

mum weight. This severely decreased manueverability and reduced speeds to around 95 knots (108 mph). Thus the UH-1B gunships found it difficult to keep up with the lighter weight and higher-performing troop-carrying choppers. This was especially true when the troop-carrying UH-1Ds started appearing in Vietnam in 1963. A faster and even more potent gunship was required.

The result was UH-1C, the first real attempt to build an integrated helicopter weapons system and not just an *ad hoc* adaptation of a troop-carrying helicopter for the gunship role. For power, a 1100-horsepower Lycoming T53-L-11 engine was used. However, the main factor contributing to UH-1C's better performance was the completely new rotor system. The blade chord width was increased to 27 inches, compared to the 15-inch and 21-inch blades used on the A and B models respectively. There was a new flexible rotor head assembly with the Bell Model 540 "door hinge" design. This gave the C model greatly improved maneuverability, almost to the point of being aerobatic. Changes to the vertical fin also helped maneuvering, as did the new synchronized elevators. The maximum cruise speed at maximum gross weight of the UH-1C was now 111 knots (126 mph). The internal fuel capacity was in-

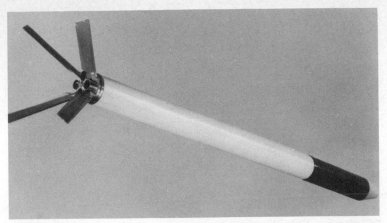

The 2.75-inch Folding Fin Aerial Rocket (FFAR) has been a popular weapon for many years. (courtesy U.S. Army)

creased from 165 to 242 gallons, allowing the range to jump to 260 nautical miles (296 miles), an increase of some 70 nautical miles (80 miles) over the B model. The easiest way to tell a C from a B model without closely examining the rotor head and tail assem-

A nineteen-tube launcher for the 2.75-inch FFAR. (courtesy Emerson Electric Co.)

The UH-1D and UH-1H versions of the Huey provided significantly greater troop and cargo-carrying capability. (courtesy Bell Helicopters Textron)

bly is by noting the location of the pitot tube and FM homing antenna. For the UH-1C they were moved to a position on the roof from their previous location on the nose.

The UH-1C was used mainly as a gunship because of its superior performance and because the Army now had a larger troop-carrying Huey, the UH-1D, which will be discussed in a bit. A typical armament package on the UH-1C was the M5 grenade launcher turret in the nose and machine guns and rocket launchers on either side, such as the M16 or M21 systems. UH-1Cs equipped with the 40mm M75 grenade launcher in the nose turret were dubbed "Frogs" because of their distinctive appearance. The M75 was given nicknames such as "Clunker," "Thumper," "Chunker," or "Blooper." If you ever heard the grenade launcher fire you would know why.

On a typical gunship mission, the UH-1Cs would go out with a crew of four—a pilot, copilot, and two door gunners. About the only protection provided against enemy fire were the lightly armored seats the pilot and copilot occupied. During a gun run, all crew members fired weapons. For example, the pilot controlled the couple of dozen 2.75-inch rockets while the copilot aimed and fired the 40mm grenade launcher with its typical 200-round load. Each

An Army UH-1H in the field. (courtesy U.S. Army)

33

Just a sample of the heavy loads the Huey is often called upon to carry. Unusual paint scheme is overall white with red nose, red/yellow/red tail bands. (courtesy U.S. Army)

door gunner was kept busy with his M60 machine gun and its 10,000 rounds of ammunition. After making a couple passes over the enemy with guns, cannons, and rockets blazing, it was time to go home to reload and refuel. With capable ground crews, this took as little as half an hour and the UH-1C and its crew could be on its way back to make some more gun runs.

Some of the UH-1Cs were retrofitted with more powerful Lycoming T53-L-13 engines rated at 1400 horsepower, making them the hottest of the Army's Hueys. These Hueys were designated UH-1Ms. Cruise speed at maximum load went up to 125 knots (143 mph), and there were significant improvements in hovering ceiling, rate-of-climb, and range. While most UH-1Cs and UH-1Ms

Maintenance crews working on a UH-1D in Vietnam. (courtesy U.S. Army)

were used as gunships, there were some slick and "dust off" versions, the latter being the commonly used term for medical evacuation missions.

Before we leave the subject of Army Huey gunships in Nam, two Hueys that became tank killers must be mentioned. In 1971, there was a new challenge in Vietnam—enemy tanks. At first, unguided rockets (such as the 2.75-incher), cannons, and the 40mm

Cockpit of a UH-1H Huey. (courtesy Bell Helicopters Textron)

Through the years, a variety of new weapons has been tested on the Huey, such as this streamlined fuselage-mounted gun pod. (courtesy U.S. Army)

grenade launcher were used against enemy armor. While destroying some tanks and other armored vehicles, it was clear that a more effective tank killer was needed. The weapon was the TOW missile,—for Tube-launched, Optically-tracked, Wire-guided. The airborne TOW missile is an adaptation of one of the Army's most

Another weapon tested on the Huey was this MiniTat machine gun. (courtesy Emerson Electric Co.)

Here a smoke generator has been added to the aft end of the engine of a UH-1H so that engineers can study airflow patterns in the engine exhaust. (courtesy U.S. Army)

successful antitank weapons; it can be fired from a variety of ground vehicles and is capable of destroying everything from bunkers to tanks.

The XM65, or TOW missile, is literally flown to the target. The copilot/gunner fires the missile and keeps his eyepiece on the target. A small red light on the missile's tail is used to track the missile in flight. A small computer aboard the launching helicopter compares the location of the missile in flight and the location

An Army UH-1D enroute to an emergency—in this case, an automobile accident. (courtesy U.S. Army)

These rubber fuel tanks can store fuel for Hueys (as well as other aircraft and surface vehicles) right in the field. (courtesy U.S. Army)

of the target and automatically computes the needed course corrections. Signals to steer the TOW on course are sent to the missile through two very thin wires, which are unreeled from the missile as it flies to the target. The TOW has a range of approxi-

A pair of Hueys doing some nap-of-the-Earth flying. (courtesy U.S. Army)

Many Hueys used in rescue operations are equipped with equipment like this so people can be hoisted from the ground.

mately 3750 meters (12,300 feet).

In order to test the airborne TOW in actual combat, two UH-1Bs were equipped with TOW launchers and sent to Vietnam in 1971. Within a short two-month period, these two Hueys had scored a rather impressive record of 65 kills including 26 tanks.

Bigger Troop Carriers

In order to meet the Army's need for a Huey that could transport more than the nominal eight troops carried on the A, B, and

Hueys equipped with TOW missiles were tested in Vietnam against enemy armored (and other) vehicles with great success. In this case, three TOWs are seen on the right stub wing; three more are mounted on the other side. (courtesy Hughes Aircraft Corp.)

C models, Bell developed the UH-1D, which became the Army's standard tactical troop carrier. The Model 205, as the whole family of larger Huey helicopters were designated by Bell, had a 3 1/2-foot longer fuselage and a 220-cubic foot internal cargo carrying capacity—an 80-cubic foot increase over the smaller Hueys. From 10 to 12 troops could now be transported into battle, depending mainly on whether they were American or Vietnamese. And when used strictly as a passenger transport, the UH-1D could be fitted with as many as 15 seats including those for the pilot and copilot. The UH-1D was fitted with two very large sliding doors that gave access to the entire cargo area, greatly facilitating loading and unloading. (The easiest way to identify the larger Model 205 helicopters is by twin windows in the cargo doors and the smaller door in front of them.)

The Model 205 had a 48-foot rotor blade with a chord of 21-inches because it was based on the technology of the UH-1B. Because of the two-foot longer rotor blade, the tail boom was extended 18 inches. The UH-1D was powered by the T53-L-11 engine, the same engine used in the UH-1C and the last of the UH-1Bs.

The first of seven YUH-1D prototypes flew in August of 1961; two years to the month later, the UH-1Ds started appearing in Vietnam, being assigned initially to the 11th Air Assault Division. Besides serving as an assault transport, the UH-1D was assigned such varied duties as command, control, and communications; reconnaissance, security, and screening; supply transport; and medical evacuation. For medevac, the UH-1D could handle six litter patients.

Starting in 1967, the D model was superceded by the UH-1H, the main change being the fitting of the 1400 horsepower T53-L-13B engine. Many of the D models were upgraded to H standards by retrofitting the more powerful engine. The UH-1D/H was a real workhorse. In addition to being able to carry 220 cubic feet of cargo internally, it could carry loads of up to 4000 pounds from the floor-mounted hook—just about the same load as could be handled inside. While the UH-1D/H 220-gallon fuel tanks allowed a range of about 250 nautical miles (285 miles), this could be extended to up to 600 nautical miles (680 miles) through the use of auxiliary tanks.

Like all Hueys, the UH-1D/H transports came equipped with hardpoints on the nose and side of the fuselage that could handle a variety of weapons. However, the U.S. Army's transports were seldom armed with more than a couple of 7.62mm or .50-caliber

Here a TOW missile is being fired from a Huey. (courtesy Hughes Aircraft Corp.)

machine guns in the doors, a flare dispenser mounted in the cargo bay, and perhaps a smoke generator.

The UH-1D and UH-1H were by far the most prolific Huey model, with nearly 8000 built. Of these, some 5,435 were H models, the majority being delivered to the U.S. Army, who in turn transferred many to the Vietnamese and Cambodians. The U.S. Army also got slightly more than 2000 of the 2,561 UH-1Ds produced.

The contributions of the Army's Huey to the Vietnam war effort is quite impressive. Between 1966 and 1971, helicopters flew about 7 1/2 million troop assault sorties and almost four million attack sorties. The "ash and trash" missions accounted for another 21 million sorties. At the peak of hostilities, the U.S. Army alone was operating 3000 helicopters in SEA. While these figures were compiled for all brands and types of helicopters, Bell-produced Hueys can be credited for at least two-thirds of these statistics. In performing these missions, about 4600 helicopters were lost in both combat and in noncombat accidents.

However, probably no story was as impressive as the one about the use of choppers in the medevac role. By war's end, some 390,000 wounded Army troops had been moved by helicopter. The result of the dust off operations can be credited with a large role in the 81-percent survival rate in Vietnam—compared to 74-percent in Korea and 71-percent in World War II. A ready supply of whole blood, highly skilled medical personnel, and well-equipped field hospitals were other important contributing factors.

Vietnam was indeed the helicopter war. The last time the U.S. Army had fought as evasive an enemy it was the American Indian. Then it was the Cavalry who engaged the enemy. In Vietnam, the cavalry horse was replaced by the helicopter.

Chapter 4

The Fighting Whirlybird

The UH-1Cs were not able to keep up with the UH-1H and the Boeing-Vertol CH-47A Chinook heavy transport helicopters that started appearing in Vietnam in the mid-1960s. What was needed was a true attack helicopter, a weapons system designed for the gunship job rather than just an armed chopper built around a troop-carrying helicopter. But this was easier said than done considering the interservice politics of the era and all the pressing needs of the U.S. Army at the time.

In the early 1960s there was a raging argument between the Army and Air Force as to how large a mission the Army's organic air support aircraft could take on without stepping into the close support mission that the USAF claimed was its role. A single-purpose armed helicopter—really a fighter helicopter—only added fuel to the argument. Even the armed helicopter advocates in the Army had a hard time visualizing—and justifying—a helicopter that had but a single purpose. The Howze Board, which was soundly in favor of the attack helicopter idea, still saw it as just one mission to be performed by a multipurpose helicopter. At the time, helicopter armament research was being given low priority and the official Army doctrine did not call for armed helicopters. In the 1960s, the Army feeling was that the gunship should be basically a utility helicopter fitted with armament packages. Then, when it was no longer needed, the armament could be removed and the helicopter returned to its utility duties. This is what it was doing

Many features, including stepped, tandem seating and the pantograph weapon sight for the gunner up front, were first introduced on the Iroquois Warrior mockup. (courtesy Bell Helicopters Textron)

with its Huey gunships. With a single-purpose armed helicopter, once it was no longer needed in combat, about all it could be used for was training.

However, Bell Helicopters was firmly convinced that the single-purpose attack helicopter was the right approach and carried on some company-funded projects that would be the forerunners of the HueyCobra when the Army decided it needed a true attack chopper. The first was the D245, called a "Combat Reconnaissance Helicopter," which was designed in 1958. It was Bell's first helicopter concept to use a narrow body that would become characteristic of attack helicopters of the future.

Next there was the D255 Iroquois Warrior, which was started in 1962 and shown to the Howze Board, where it met with considerable interest. The Iroquis Warrior had many features—such as stepped tandem seating, narrow, low-drag fuselage, nose gun turret, and stub wings at mid-fuselage—that would be keys to the HueyCobra's success. The narrow tandem fuselage had several advantages. The smaller profile decreased drag, improved handling, and made a smaller target for enemy detection and gunfire. Having the pilot sitting behind and above the gunner gave both crew

Originally, the Army had set its sights on the AH-56A Cheyenne as its attack helicopter of the future. The Cheyenne was really half helicopter, half fixed-wing airplane with its aircraft-like wings and pusher tail propeller. (courtesy Lockheed-California Company)

The Model 207 Sioux Scout demonstrated concepts that would be incorporated into the HueyCobra. (courtesy Bell Helicopters Textron)

members almost unlimited visibility. Like the HueyCobras that would follow, the Iroquois Warrior was designed around UH-1 componentry. Unfortunately, this Warrior never got beyond the wooden mockup stage.

However, one early company-funded attack helicopter concept did fly. This was the Model 207 Sioux Scout. This prototype, started in late 1962, was based on the Bell OH-13 to keep costs low, but used many of the design features introduced on the Iroquois Warrior. It was powered by a supercharged piston engine; the rotor assembly came from the OH-13, and the tail rotor, transmission, center section, and tail rotor were from Bell's Model 47 commercial helicopter. There was tandem seating for the pilot and gunner, a remotely controlled Emerson chin turret with two M60 machine guns, and stub wings with rocket pods mounted on them. The forward fuselage used honeycomb panelling over a box beam construction, just as later used on the HueyCobra. This structural technique served as the mounting for the chin turret, and as such, minimized vibration and absorbed the recoil of the turret guns.

The Model 207 had one of the first pantograph weapon sights, which was used by the gunner for sighting and firing the machine guns. As in all Bell attack helicopters, the gunner occupied the front seat. The fuselage was a mere 39-inches wide, although it looked wider because of the Sioux Scout's short overall length. Equipped with a piston engine, it had a top speed of only 110-knots (125-mph), much too slow for an effective attack helicopter.

While never destined for production, Bell engineers and the Army learned a lot about attack helicopters in some 300 hours of flight testing (starting in July 1963) that was done with the single Sioux Scout, much of which would be useful in the design of the HueyCobra, which started in 1964. It was demonstrated at virtually every major Army base in the U.S., the 11th Air Assault Division even went as far as recommending that it go into development except it should be powered by a turbine engine.

The Sioux Scout flying in the attack helicopter's natural environment—in amongst the trees and bushes, performing nap-of-the-Earth maneuvers. (courtesy Bell Helicopters Textron)

The HueyCobra was extensively tested in the wind tunnel in order to improve its aerodynamics and thus its performance. (courtesy U.S. Army)

It is hard to believe that this HueyCobra shares much of the componentry with the Huey transports and gunships. It's the sleek fuselage that makes much of the difference—not only in looks, but also in performance. (courtesy Bell Helicopters Textron)

N209J was the prototype for the HueyCobra. It was the only HueyCobra to use retractable landing skids, shown here in their extended position. (courtesy Patton Museum)

Meanwhile, the U.S. Army had more grandiose ideas about what it wanted in an attack helicopter when it put out its requirements for its Advanced Aerial Fire Support System (AAFSS) to the industry in 1964. The result was the Lockheed AH-56 Cheyenne and a Sikorsky design based on the technology from its S-67 Blackhawk program. The Army's requirements were quite demanding, as can be seen by the specifications for the Cheyenne, the winner of the competition between Lockheed and Sikorsky. For starters, the AH-56 had a top speed of almost 245 knots (280 mph) in a shallow dive, and 215 knots (245 mph) in straight and level

Engineers and technicians preparing N209J for another flight test. (courtesy Patton Museum)

flight at altitudes ranging from on-the-deck to 20,000 feet. To accomplish this, the Cheyenne was a compound helicopter; that is, in addition to a rotor it had a reversible-pitch pusher propeller for fast forward flight. Also needed were the small fixed wings. In reality, the Cheyenne was more of a fixed-wing fighter than a helicopter. The rotor was there for takeoffs, landings, hovering, and low-speed flight. At high speeds, the propeller and wings did most of the work, with the rotor main and tail providing control. The requirements in AAFSS program called for the Cheyenne to be able to ferry itself over a distance of 2,100 nautical miles (2400 miles), the overwater distance from California to Hawaii.

Much advanced technology for its day, such as a centralized computer, hingeless rotor, advanced control system, and infrared night vision system, was planned. This sophisticated attack helicopter would not be ready for deployment until the late 1960s at best, and eventually was cancelled when costs got out of hand and because of political pressures. What the Army needed was an interim attack helicopter to meet current Vietnam requirements. As for the future attack helicopter, the Army rated survivability in combat over high speed.

By 1965, the war in Vietnam was escalating, especially with

respect to Army aviation's role. At that time General William Westmoreland advised the Pentagon that the war had reached the point where either the AAFSS had to become available immediately or an interim solution found. The decision was made to continue the long-range AAFSS development and to look for an off-the-shelf solution for the immediate need for an armed helicopter.

In August 1965, a committee was convened to study the currently available helicopters to see how they could be modified to meet the urgent requirements. The five aircraft considered were the Sikorsky S-61A with armament replacing the floatation gear; the Kaman UH-2 Tomahawk; the Boeing Vertol ACH-47A with its 2000 pounds of armor, external weapons, and five gunners; the Piasecki Model 16H compound helicopter; and the Bell Model 209.

Bell Model 209

The Model 209 was another Bell-sponsored development of an attack helicopter, which the company started when it lost out on the AAFSS competition. Originally called the Model D262, the design and construction, started in March 1965, was guided by Bell engineer J.P. Duppstadt. The design combined the features tested

The gunner up front and the pilot in the rear have tremendous visibility in the HueyCobra. (courtesy Bell Helicopters Textron)

HueyCobras like this one first saw action in Vietnam in the summer of 1967. (courtesy Patton Museum)

on the Sioux Scout and already proven in combat on the UH-1C gunships.

From the Model 207 came features such as stepped tandem seating, stub wings, and remote-control turret. The UH-1C contributed the high-performance Bell 540 rotor system and cambered vertical fin as well as most of the major internal dynamic components. To further reduce drag, the familiar stabilizer bar on the rotor was eliminated. The electronic Stability and Control Augmentation System (SCAS) took its place. From experience with Huey gunships in Vietnam, Bell emphasized low vibration, good visibility, aerodynamic efficiency, structural integrity, and maintainability in the design of the Model 209.

While Bell did consider a compound design using an auxiliary propeller or turbojet engine, the idea was discarded because it was rightfully felt that a pure helicopter was quite capable of meeting the intended speed range of less than 200 knots (228-mph) in a dive. Another original idea was to use retractable landing gear. However, when the slight speed increase was weighed against increased maintenance and safety risks such as landing with the gear retracted, the idea was discarded. The HueyCobra, like all the Hueys, would retain Bell's familiar skid-type landing system. However, the HueyCobra prototype did have retractable gear.

Another feature of the Model 209 and all subsequent Huey-Cobras was the stub wings. These gave increased manueverability because they allowed partial rotor unloading at high speeds, where they provided some additional aerodynamic lift. They improved handling qualities, making it seem more like flying a fixed-wing aircraft. Finally, they provided weapons pylons for holding the HueyCobra's vast array of weapons. Each wing was equipped with two pylons.

The Model 209 first flew on September 7, 1965, just six months after construction started. This first flying prototype was given the registration number N209J and would see 1090 hours of test flying and demonstration before it was retired in 1971 and subsequently donated to the Patton Museum of Cavalry and Armor at Fort Knox, Kentucky. In its day, N209J carried hundreds of people, including admirals, generals, and heads of state during demonstrations, including those in 10 foreign countries.

By November 1965, the Model 209 was in "comparative" testing against the two remaining contenders for the interim attack helicopter job, the Sikorsky S-61A and the Kaman UH-2. Based on a two-month test program at Edwards AFB, California, the Army chose the Bell design. By April 1966, a contract had been signed

HueyCobras were often painted for added effect. This sharkmouthed gunship has just fired a 2.75-inch rocket at a Vietcong position. (courtesy U.S. Army)

The HueyCobra shown with two of its close cousins in the background. Immediately behind it is a UH-1B, and above that, a UH-1D. (courtesy Bell Helicopters Textron)

for two prototypes, and only nine days later the Army ordered 100 production Bell 209s.

Originally, the Model 209 was given the Army designation UH-1H, but this was changed to the AH-1G within a few months, the UH-1H being assigned to the improved troop carrier Huey. The name Cobra was generically applied to all gunships in Vietnam, so the AH-1G was officially called the HueyCobra. It is the only Army helicopter that does not have an Indian name somewhere in its official designation. Gunships and attack helicopters were also referred to as "snakes" in Vietnam. For Bell, the name Cobra also has significant historical meaning. The famous Bell P-39 and P-63 of World War II fame were called, respectively, the AiraCobra and KingCobra.

The HueyCobra

The Army favored the Bell 209 for two principal reasons. First, being based on the Huey, it could be placed in production rapidly. Even more importantly, it could be deployed into the field quickly—just 18 months after the contract go-ahead date. Commonality with the Hueys meant it could share much of the existing parts inventory, and maintenance crews could service the HueyCobra with little or no retraining.

Secondly, there was the design itself. Powered by the Lycoming T-53-L-13 1400-horsepower engine, the AH-1G has a maximum cruise speed of over 150 knots (171 mph), and 190 knots (216 mph) in a shallow dive. Thus it had no trouble flying escort for any of the modern troop-carrying transport helicopters. Since the AH-1G used the Bell 540 door hinge rotor head assembly, it has outstanding maneuverability. Even though weighing essentially the same as the Hueys, it could go faster because of its 36-inch-wide, slimline design. With the two-man crew—versus the four men required to effectively operate a Huey gunship—there was more capacity

A typical scene in Vietnam, a HueyCobra escorting two Huey troopships. (courtesy U.S. Army)

The HueyCobra's turret, showing the 7.62mm minigun on the left and the 40mm grenade launcher on the right. (courtesy Bell Helicopters Textron)

to carry ordnance. In the Cobra, the pilot sits in the rear seat and the copilot/gunner sits up front. With this arrangement, the rear seat is elevated above the front seat; the pilot has better control and the copilot/gunner can fire the HueyCobra's many weapons more accurately. Both crewmen have excellent visibility through the bubble cockpit.

Then there are the HueyCobra's weapons. Originally the AH-1G, like the prototype Model 209, was fitted with an Emerson Electric Company hydraulically driven TAT 102 turret with a single General Electric 7.62mm minigun. The ammunition bay aft of the turret had a capacity of 8000 rounds. The pantograph weapons sight used by the gunner included triggers and turret activation switches. The gunner could direct the turret through 230 degrees of azimuth, 15 to 25 degrees of elevation and 50 degrees of depression. The pilot could also fire the turret gun, but only when it was in its stowed forward position. He aimed the gun by aiming the aircraft itself.

The TAT 102 turret was subsequently replaced by the M28 Turret, also made by Emerson Electric, which carried dual weapons, a six-barreled 7.62mm minigun firing up to 4000 rounds per minute and a 40mm grenade launcher that could fire up to 400 rounds per minute. Many different combinations of ordnance could be carried on the four pylons beneath the HueyCobra's stubby wings. Some of these include rocket pods holding up to 19 2.75-inch Folding Fin Aerial Rockets, a 7.62mm minigun, or a six-barreled 20mm cannon. Again, the turret weapons were controlled by the copilot/gunner with the pilot able to fire them only when in the stowed position. The turret returned to the stowed position whenever the gunner released his grip on the turret slewing switch. The pilot's job, when things got hot, was firing the weapons on the two stores stations on each of the stub wings. When equipped with the full complement of four rocket pods with 19 2.75-inch rockets each, the troops in the field referred to a HueyCobra as being armed with "76 trombones." The gunner could also fire the wing stores.

While the HueyCobra derived most of its ability to survive in combat from its speed, agility, and small profile, the AH-1G was fitted with some armor plating in key locations. For example, dual hardness armor provides protection for the structure as well as the crew. The crew's side armor panels are made of boron carbide, but the crew wears armored vests for forward protection. Armor protection is provided for such components as the engine fuel controls and engine compressor. Fuel tanks are self-sealing. Many parts

This disassembled HueyCobra shows that much of it is basically rather simple. (courtesy Bell Helicopters Textron)

This is the instrument panel for the HueyCobra pilot. (courtesy Bell Helicopters Textron)

of the HueyCobra were designed to take a .30-caliber hit and survive.

HueyCobras in Vietnam

After 16 months of extensive flight testing, the first production HueyCobra was delivered to the Army's New Equipment Training Team. Within four more months the first AH-1G appeared in Vietnam—and what an appearance it made. On September 4, 1967, the HueyCobra was credited with its first kill in Vietnam. Major General George Seneff, commander of the First Aviation Brigade, destroyed a Viet Cong sampan on the Mekong Delta. But the AH-1G really got to show its stuff during the January 1968 Tet Offensive. Here it played a key role in blunting the enemy's costly offensive. The Cobra's guns and rockets were used many times to flush out the enemy and provide suppressive fire that allowed troops pinned down by the enemy to escape.

The HueyCobra also rode shotgun for troop-carrying choppers, a job it inherited from the older Huey gunships such as the UH-1B/C. Another use of the AH-1G was as part of a "Pink Team" consisting of a HueyCobra and an OH-6A observation helicopter.

The OH-6A would reconnoiter enemy positions and Viet Cong escape routes while the AH-1G provided protective cover, and when possible, engaged the enemy.

The attack helicopter had a capability that was unmatched by few other weapon systems in the U.S. inventory. It could detect battlefield targets and immediately engage them, even when the targets were in close proximity to friendly troops. It could also operate in poor weather conditions and low ceilings, when the Air Force's and Navy's close support aircraft could not fly. The HueyCobras were also used to locate targets and direct fire for the artillery and for tactical air strikes. After the strikes, the AH-1Gs would return to assess the damage.

While the AH-1Gs usually flew at 1500 feet, its guns were accurate at altitudes up to 4000. However, the key to the HueyCobra's effectiveness is its ability to survive in battle, especially from small arms ground fire. There are two parts to the survival equation: first, to avoid detection; second, if detected, to survive enemy hits. The HueyCobra's very slim forward profile made it a difficult target to detect and track. Helicopter pilots soon found the best way to avoid detection was to fly so low that the enemy could not detect their presence until after they had attacked. Attack helicopter pilots—and for that matter, gunship pilots, too—fly their choppers

This is where the copilot/gunner works. (courtesy Bell Helicopters Textron)

Details of the rotor head of the AH-1G.

following the contours of the Earth at altitudes measured in tens of feet using dikes, small hills, rock formations, clumps of trees, and bushes to mask their presence. This type of flying has been given the title nap-of-the-Earth or NOE for short. NOE flying is very demanding for both the crews and the helicopters, but the HueyCobras were up to the task, as were the pilots. Once the attack chopper pilot sights his target, he pops up only long enough

The rotor head on the Huey, in this case a UH-1H.

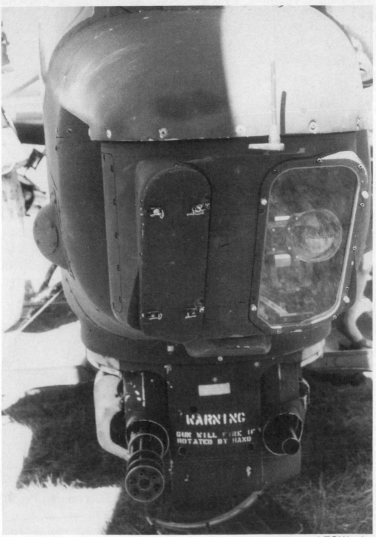

The Telescopic Sighting Unit used to fire the turret weapons and TOW missiles would be housed here. Below are the turret weapons.

to fire his weapons; this usually takes about a half-minute. Then he drops back down again to hide.

Among the threats Army helicopters faced in Vietnam was the Soviet-made SAM-7 infrared-seeking missile, which homes in on an aircraft's hot exhaust. When the SAM-7 began taking its toll of AH-1GS and UH-1s, the Army came up with a quick fix. This consisted of a shield that directed the engine's hot exhaust into the

Details of the TOW missile launchers. Next to them is a seven-tube launcher for the 2.75-inch folding fin rockets.

wash of the rotor, where it was dispersed rather than being concentrated in the normal engine exhaust stream. While the solution did represent a weight penalty, it did help defeat the SAM-7 threat.

There were other running changes made during the production of AH-1GS, which resulted from combat experiences in Vietnam. If you compare the tail rotor location on early AH-1Gs with later models, you will find that it has been switched. Early models had it on the left side, and it was found that the pilot ran out of yaw control—especially in side winds and when backing up. All Hueys had this problem to some extent, but it was especially pronounced on the HueyCobras with their taller tails. The changes were made at the factory during production, and sometimes right in the field in Vietnam.

Also during the war, the chin turret was changed from the single gun TAT-102 to the M28, which could handle two weapons. Air conditioning was added to the cockpit to handle the stifling heat of the SEA jungles—which was compounded by the AH-1G's canopy. There was a price to pay for excellent visibility.

Tank Killers

Since the Vietnamese war, the military's attention has been focused on the more conventional type of warfare, such as might be faced on an Eastern European battlefield. The experts all realize that if we have to go up against the Warsaw Pact nations, we will have to fight greatly outnumbered. These countries can mount an attack with more tanks, artillery weapons, mortars, and troops than the U.S. and its European allies. One of the equalizers in this arena is the helicopter tank killer.

As discussed in Chapter 3, TOW-carrying UH-1Cs were successfully tested in Vietnam, but on a limited scale. The first true U.S. tank-killing helicopter was the Army's AH-1Q. However, before getting to the AH-1Q, mention should be made of Bell's Model 309 KingCobra, another company-sponsored program that would contribute to the Army's AH-1Q.

The KingCobra, while basically a HueyCobra, had a fuselage that was stretched to 49 feet and a 48-foot diameter rotor with high-lift, low-drag characteristics and a 33-inch chord. There was a ventral tail below the normal tail for added yaw control. Power came from a Lycoming T-55-L-7C engine that was rated at 2850 horsepower. The transmission was beefed up to handle the additional power, being rated at 2050 horsepower for takeoff and 1800 horsepower for continuous operation. The AH-1G's transmission was rated at only 1100 horsepower continuous, by comparison. The wingspan was increased by over two feet to 13 feet to permit a larger fuel capacity and more space to carry external stores. The

The engine exhaust deflector deflects the exhaust into the wake of the rotor to reduce the infrared signature.

The helmet-mounted sight is mounted over this crewman's right eye.

KingCobra had a gross weight of 14,000 pounds, 4500 more than the AH-1G.

However, its biggest advances were made in the area of weapons and electronics. For example, the KingCobra had night vision capability provided by its Low Light Level Television (LLLTV) and Forward Looking Infrared (FLIR) sensors, the latter being the reason for the KingCobra's distinctive elongated nose. Other sophisticated gear included an inertial guidance system, Head-Up Display (HUD), helmet-mounted and stabilized multi-sensor sights, fire control computer, and guidance and electronics for the TOW missile. In addition to eight TOW missiles, the King-Cobra could be armed with 2.75-inch rocket pods, and either a 20mm or 30mm gun was mounted in the chin turret. The King-Cobra made its first flight in January 1972 and was Bell's entry in the fly-off for the Army's AAFSS program, which included the Sikorsky Blackhawk and the Lockheed Cheyenne. As we know, none of these attack helicopters ever got into production, but the KingCobra did in a way get the furthest in the form of the modifications made for the AH-1Q.

In January 1974, Bell Helicopters was given an Army contract to modify just over 100 AH-1Gs to fire the TOW missile; these were designated AH-1Q. Bell had already converted eight AH-1Gs to TOW launchers under the Improved Cobra Armament Program (ICAP) sponsored by the Army. These early TOW-equipped

AH-1Qs were used in Vietnam in the concluding days of U.S. involvement with rather impressive results, even though the hot and high-altitude environment in Vietnam limited the number of TOWs that could be carried on a mission. Although Bell was initially contracted to convert a total of 290 AH-1Gs, only about a hundred AH-1Qs were actually built because the AH-1Gs were needed for another modification program that provided a more potent tank killer, as we will see in a bit.

Except for the TOW-related equipment, the AH-1Gs and AH-1Qs are almost identical in terms of airframe and propulsion systems. Thus, the performance of the AH-1Q remained essentially the same as the AH-1G. The bulk of the funds for the program went into the TOW missile and the equipment to fire it. The Hughes-built TOW system consists of a telescopic stabilized sight, sight hand control, and pilot's steering indicator, plus the wing mounted launchers. There is also a myriad of controls, displays, and electronic componentry to fire the TOW and guide it to the target. Both the pilot and the copilot/gunner stations are equipped with helmet sights.

To operate the TOW system, the gunner acquires and tracks the target while the pilot aligns the helicopter in the needed prelaunch envelope using the steering indicator. When the gunner has fired a TOW, the pilot is then free to maneuver the helicopter

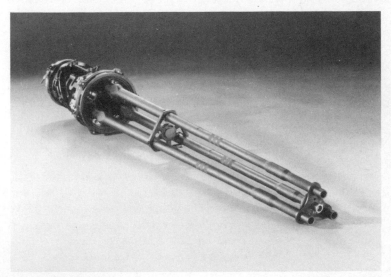

The Gatling-type 20mm cannon used on the AH-1S version of the HueyCobra. (courtesy General Electric)

An AH-1Q TOW-equipped HueyCobra during development testing. (courtesy U.S. Army)

within certain limits, as shown on his sight, allowing him to fly some limited evasive maneuvers while the TOW is in flight. While the missile is in flight, the gunner keeps his sights on the target. He needs only to track the target to achieve a hit. The TOW has a range of 3750 meters—over two miles—and can pierce tank hulls at that range, being able to knock out a tank on the first shot without the typical "bracketing" rounds formerly needed, which quickly disclose the gunner's position. The TOW is also used by Army ground units, being mounted on a variety of vehicles from Jeeps to armored personnel carriers, and can even be hand-carried.

The TOW missile itself is some 117 centimeters (46 inches) long, 15 centimeters (5.9 inches) in diameter, and weighs 19 kilograms (42 pounds). There are three versions of the TOW—the basic version, the improved or I TOW, and the TOW 2. The I TOW has an improved warhead to increase its ability to penetrate armor, while the TOW 2's warhead is even further improved to defeat even more advanced enemy armor. The guidance system for the TOW 2 is also improved so it can be more accurately guided through battlefields clouded with smoke and dust in day or night.

AH-1S Series

Before the Army proceeded very far with the production of

AH-1Q, it decided that what it really wanted was an even more capable tank killer—one that could carry a full complement of TOW missiles under all environmental conditions and be more survivable on the battlefield. Thus the AH-1S was born. Actually, the fielding of the AH-1S series of anti-armor helicopters has been a multi-step process.

The uprating program started with three evaluation configurations. First, the YAG-1Qs were the eight early TOW-equipped AH-1Gs mentioned previously under the ICAP designation. Secondly, the YAH-1R was a single AH-1G modified for greater performance through the use of an 1800-horsepower T53-L-703 engine and an improved transmission and drivetrain components. The performance improvements were titled Improved Cobra Agility and Manueverability, or ICAM. The YAH-1R had no TOW missile carrying capability. Finally, there was one YAH-1S, a YAH-1Q with the same performance improvements as the YAH-1R, but with TOW capability.

From these prototypes, Bell and the Army went ahead first with the "Modified" AH-1S, or MOD S HueyCobra. The MOD S models were some 378 AH-1Gs that were upgraded by structural strengthening, ICAM performance improvements, and, most importantly, provision for the TOW missile. Incidentally, Bell and Dornier of

An AH-1Q equipped with TOW missile launchers. (courtesy U.S. Army)

West Germany converted some 62 AH-1Gs based in Europe that had already been converted to AH-1Qs to the Mod S configuration. While these conversions were made in the 1970s, about 30 more AH-1G conversions were ordered in 1984.

Then there are the TH-1Ss, 10 Mod AH-1S HueyCobras used to train pilots on the Forward-Looking Infrared (FLIR) night vision system built by Martin-Marietta, and the Integrated Helmet and Display Sighting System (IHADSS) built by Honeywell. The TH-1S also has such sophisticated equipment as a Pilot's Night Vision Sensor (PNVS) and blue instrument lighting for easier reading with night vision goggles. Appropriately, this modification program is called Night Stalker; the FLIR, IHADSS, and PNVS are not equipment found on the HueyCobras, but on the Army's newest attack helicopter, the AH-64 Apache. Thus the TH-1S will be used to train Apache crews.

The AH-1Ss of greatest interest to the Army, however, were the Production S models, AH-1Ss built with all new airframes. The first 100 Production AH-1Ss were delivered to the Army in 1977 and 1978. Besides the upgraded performance found on the Mod S AH-1S, the Production AH-1S had many features to increase its survivability on the battlefield. The most noticeable change was the flat-windowed canopy, which reduced the sun glint that occurs with curved canopies and is a giveaway to the enemy that a chopper is operating in the area. The instrument panel was revised to facilitate nap-of-the-Earth flying, and new avionics were added. Production AH-1Ss produced after the 66th one had a new main rotor blade, made of composite materials, that was more capable of taking an enemy hit and surviving to get the HueyCobra back home. The first Production AH-1S were delivered to the 82nd Airborne Division at Fort Bragg, North Carolina, in August 1977.

After the 100th new AH-1S had been produced, the "Up-Gun" version of the Production AH-1S starting rolling off the Bell assembly line. As the title implies, the main changes were in the helicopter's armament. A universal turret made by General Electric allows the interchangeability of either an XM197 20mm Gatling gun, which can fire 750 rounds per minute, or an XM230 30mm Chain gun, capable of more than 700 rounds per minute. A new Wing Store Management System for the 2.75-inch rocket system allows the crew to choose warhead and fuse types, firing intervals, and single or multiple rocket firing. Onboard equipment also provides automatic compensation for off-axis firing of the guns. A more powerful alternator and improvements to the flight controls were

The latest of the HueyCobras, the AH-1S is easily distinguished by its flat glass canopy. (courtesy U.S. Army)

added to go along with the armament improvements. Ninety-eight Up-Gun AH-1Ss were delivered to the Army in 1978 and 1979.

After the 199th Production AH-1S, a new version was introduced, the Modernized AH-1S. This model has all the previously mentioned improvements, plus a lot more. For starters, the pilot has a Head-Up Display (HUD), plus a fire control system that includes a ballistics computer, low-airspeed sensor, and laser rangefinder and tracker, all to improve the accuracy of both the cannon and rocket weapon systems. Other improved avionics include a stabilized sight, air data system, solid-state IFF transponder for telling friend from foe, and Doppler navigation system. The Modernized AH-1S has much equipment to decrease detectability, including a suppressor to reduce the infrared signature from the engine's hot metal parts and its exhaust plume as well as an infrared jammer. Like all the later HueyCobras, the Modernized AH-1S is painted with a special anti-infrared paint scheme. One important piece of this attack helicopter's avionics is a radar warning receiver, which provides the pilot with both visual and sound warning when an enemy radar is beamed on the aircraft. A total of 99 Modernized AG-1Ss have been delivered to the U.S. Army, and the Army National Guard is eventually to be equipped with another 50 more.

But even with these AH-1Ss, the end of the HueyCobra's life is not in sight. Bell is still looking at further improvements, such as its Model 249 Cobra/TOW 2 program. This model incorporates the four-bladed rotor system from the Model 412 commercial Huey, a lengthened tailboom, and higher thrust tail rotor. Equipped with the TOW 2 missile and Forward Looking Infrared (FLIR) system, the Model 249 makes a very capable night fighter.

While the Army's Apache is the most advanced fighter helicopter in the Army's inventory, the HueyCobra will still play an important role in supporting ground forces and for anti-armor warfare for a long time into the future.

Chapter 5

Marine Corps Hueys

The United States Marine Corps was a leader in the use of helicopters as battlefield weapons, starting with the armed CH-19s during the Korean War. The Marine Corps thought about arming the helicopter almost from the day in 1948 it got its first two fragile Sikorsky H03S observation helicopters. Way back in 1949, a Marine Corps visionary even forecasted their use in an anti-armor role. But early experiments with armed helicopters were disappointing. The fledgling choppers were too unstable and limited in lift capacity to make them decent gun platforms. The Marine Corps did send observers to Algeria, where the French were having moderate success with helicopters armed with guns, bazookas, and missiles.

In 1959, the Marine Corps again tested firing weapons from helicopters. First, it tried a French made SS-11 wire-guided air-to-surface missile. Then 2.75-inch rockets and 20mm cannons were considered. In 1960, 600-pound Bullpup missiles were successfully fired from a UH-34 and "flown" to the target with excellent accuracy.

USMC Helicopters in Vietnam

Marine Corps helicopters appeared in Vietnam in the spring of 1962,when a squadron of UH-34s landed at Soc Trang in the Delta region to begin Operation Shufly. At first, these choppers were essentially unarmed. The Marines believed that a machine

The Marine Corps' UH-1E was essentially identical to the Army's UH-1B except for equipment needed to meet the Marines' particular needs. (courtesy Bell Helicopters Textron)

gun mounted in the door would obstruct and slow down the exiting troops. The copilot and crew chief were given hand-held machine guns. The main defensive tactic at that time was to spend the minimum time possible on the ground. The results were far from optimal.

By the fall of 1962, an M60 machine gun was mounted in the UH-34's doorway and the copilot and crew chief had automatic rifles to fire from the cockpit and cabin. The crew was given some protection by way of special flak suits, and later by lightweight armored seats. Interestingly, the rules of engagement at the time called for the Marines to fire only if shot at first. Fortunately, this rule lost something in its transmission to the field.

In March 1963, three UH-34s from the Shufly Squadron provided the first Marine Corps close air support from a helicopter. By May 1964, another M60 door gun was added to the UH-34. This still did not provide the firepower the Marines really needed. Besides, the weight of arms and armor on the UH-34 was eating into the payload capacity of the UH-34, thus hindering the chopper's main mission, assault troop transport. What was really needed was a helicopter specifically designed to carry weapons and fight.

The Marine Corps UH-1Es operated much of the time from ships based at sea, and some changes had to be made such as the addition of a rotor brake and substitution of aluminum for magnesium to survive the harsh salt-water environment. (courtesy U.S. Navy)

The Marines' use of rotary-wing gunships lagged by some time the Army's employment. There were several reasons for this lag, even though many Corps members saw the potential of the armed helicopter much earlier. First of all, the Army was prohibited from

Two UH-1Es about to land on the *USS Denver* after performing gunfire spotting mission in the Gulf of Tonkin. (courtesy U.S. Marine Corps)

having any armed fixed-wing aircraft. That was the Air Force's, Navy's, and Marine Corps' bailiwick. Thus, if the Army was to have any airborne firepower of its own, it would have to be based on helicopters. This was not the case for the USMC, which had its own fixed-wing close support fighters and well-developed tactics for escorting troop-carrying transports. The helicopter, in the eyes of many Marine leaders, was strictly for troop and supply transport. Opponents of armed helicopters within the Marine Corps believed fixed-wing aircraft to be superior to the slower, more vulnerable, and less stable helicopter.

The biggest opposition came, however, from the fact that the USMC feared that by classifying its armed helicopters as attack aircraft and using them as attack fighters, Congress and the Department of Defense would count them as attack machines, thereby limiting the number of fixed-wing high-performance attack aircraft in the USMC's inventory. Indeed, that fear of losing jet-powered fixed-wing aircraft to armed helicopters became almost a paranoia for Marine Corps leaders in the early stages of the Vietnam war.

Once in Vietnam, it did not take the Marine Corps long to realize the potential of the helicopter for the unique fighting conditions found there. USMC doctrine called for attack aircraft, naval gunfire, and artillery fire to secure a safe landing zone for helicopter-borne assault troops. This was difficult in Vietnam, where the bad guys were intermingled with the good guys. Air strikes with almost surgical precision were needed to suppress the enemy without doing harm to friendly troops and the civilian population. The Marines—especially those experienced in the Shufly Operation—recognized that the armed helicopter was just the weapon to do the job. It could fly low and slow, and even hover, while firing its weapons.

To improve the situation somewhat, the armed UH-34s were fitted with armament kits consisting of two rocket pods and two machine guns pods, all mounted on a platform located just above the landing gear. These armed UH-34s did not turn out to be great gunships. The 1000 pounds of armament greatly reduced troop and cargo-carrying capacity and the armed UH-34 was very vulnerable to enemy gunfire. Experience showed that while the armed UH-34s accounted for only 15 percent of the total UH-34 flight time, they were taking 85 percent of the hits. A better gunship was needed, and the Marines turned to the Hueys, a proven vehicle. Incidentally, starting in 1963, some of the Army Huey gunships rode shotgun for Marine Corps' UH-34s on assault missions.

All the services purchased the twin-engined UH-1N. This is the USMC version. (courtesy Bell Helicopters Textron)

The Marine Corps finally got its first armed Hueys in February 1964, and a year later they went to work in Vietnam. The Marines' gunship was the UH-1E, which was essentially identical to the Army's UH-1B, being powered by the 1100-horsepower T53-1-11 engine. There were changes in radios, electrical systems, and avionics to standardize them with Navy and Marine Corps procedures. One of the important differences between the Army and Marine Hueys was a rotor brake on the Marine versions. This was vitally needed for amphibious operations. On the flight deck of a ship there is no room to have the rotor gradually come to a stop. In these close quarters, the rotor must be stopped immediately. (These brakes also prevent the rotors from whirling in the breeze aboard the ships.) Another important difference was the use of aluminum rather than magnesium in the various components of the UH-1E. While heavier, aluminum does not corrode as easily in the harsh environment at sea. Also, it does not burn violently as does magnesium.

Like their Army counterparts, the Marine UH-1Es were assigned a myriad of tasks. Marine slicks were used for liaison, command and control, courier, and supply duties. Others were used for visual reconnaissance and observation, and—with sophisticated equipment installed—as platforms for aerial searchlights and special sensors. No small task was the transportation of VIPs around the battlefront. Of course, a primary job was transporting troops to and from the action.

The Marine Hueys—indeed, all Marine choppers—played a key role in medevac of battle casualties. Often the wounded were evacuated not by specifically equipped choppers with hospital corpsman aboard, but just by the helicopter that happened to be the closest to the casualty. The number of medevac missions flown by USMC helicopters was impressive. In 1968, a peak year, nearly 67,000 people were evacuated in just under 47,000 sorties. And a great many of these were done under heavy ground fire with the rescuing choppers taking hits and casualties themselves. For example, on a night rescue with troops in contact with the enemy, flare aircraft would circle and illuminate the pickup zone. Helicopter gunships and ground support fighters would provide fire suppression. The evacuation helicopter would then go in and make the pickup using whatever natural concealment might be available.

Flying helicopters was a dirty job. As a group, Marine helicopter crews were awarded a large percentage of Purple Hearts for wounds sustained in combat.

Not all military Huey missions were warlike. This UH-1N brought Santa Claus to visit schoolchildren on the island of Okinawa. (courtesy U.S. Marine Corps)

The Marines liked the idea of an attack helicopter. Here, N209J, the original HueyCobra prototype, is being closely examined by some Naval and Marine Corps aviators. (courtesy U.S. Navy)

The Marine UH-1Es armed as gunships perhaps had the most dangerous job. Originally the UH-1E was procured as an unarmed transport, and when the UH-1Es were first armed it was for self-defense. There was still strong sentiment about the use of armed helicopters versus traditional fixed-wing close-support aircraft. The point of arming the UH-1Es was to give them some measure of protection during unescorted observation, reconnaissance, and medical evacuation missions on the front lines.

At first, the UH-1Es were equipped with what the Marine Corps called the TK-2, or Temporary Kit-2, an armament package similar to that used on the UH-34s. The TK-2 system consisted of two M60C machine guns attached to the Huey's fuselage hardpoints. Bomb racks were located below the guns. This armament placement resulted in the guns being fixed in a forward firing position, in contrast to the UH-1B's crew-controlled, movable guns, which gave a more flexible gun system. The result was that the Marines had to develop and use entirely different tactics than the Army in employing their Huey gunships. Also, Marine transport helicopter pilots who had worked with the Army's gunships were very disenchanted with the Marines' fixed gun system. Beginning in 1967, the situation improved greatly when the UH-1Es were fitted with

Four of the single-engined AH-1Gs used by the Marine Corps before they got their SeaCobras. (courtesy Bell Helicopters Textron)

The SeaCobra during some early test flights. (courtesy Bell Helicopters Textron)

Emerson TAT-101 chin turrets equipped with twin M60 machine guns, which were controlled by the pilot. Other armament used on the UH-1Es included 2.75-inch rocket pods and .30-caliber machine guns in the doors.

Well over 200 UH-1Es were built between 1964 and 1968, along with a score of TH-1E training versions. The UH-1E turned out to be a very good gunship—perhaps *too* good. As previously mentioned, it was originally intended for slick missions, but due to the combination of the frequent lack of available fixed-wing close-support aircraft, the UH-1E's effectiveness, and its ability to fly under conditions that kept fixed-wing fighters on the ground, almost two-thirds of the UH-1E missions were as armed gunships in support of ground troops.

Typical of how the Marines integrated its UH-1Es with its other tactical air resources were the Super Gaggle missions to supply hill outposts in the Khe Sanh area. Every helicopter flight to the outposts was extremely hazardous because of a heavy concentration of enemy antiaircraft weapons. Added to this was monsoon weather, requiring instrument flying. On a Super Gaggle mission, the CH-46A transport helicopters met up with their escort of UH-1Es gunships and A-4 fighters. The gunships and fighters would work over the area with napalm, rockets, 20mm guns, and smoke before the CH-46As would land and deposit their loads (within five minutes). The whole operation would be controlled by an airborne Tactical Air Controller in a two-seat TA-4F.

Marine Attack Helicopters

The Marine Corps watched the development of the Army's HueyCobra with intense interest. They saw that by buying AH-1s they would be able to free up their UH-1Es for their intended transport and support missions. In early 1969, the USMC got its first 38 AH-1Gs. This was such a small number of aircraft that instead of training its own pilots, the Marine Corps sent potential Huey-Cobra pilots to the Army's flight school at Fort Rucker, Alabama. In March 1969, when the first four Marine pilots graduated, they stood numbers one through four out of 154 students in their class.

The first Marine HueyCobras reached Vietnam in April 1969 and went to work within a few days, their first mission riding shotgun for a medical evacuation flight. As expected, the AH-1G proved to be much better gun platform than the UH-1E. It had more firepower with greater accuracy, higher cruise speeds, and could dive more steeply during an attack. Not only could it keep up with the

The launcher for the 2.75-inch folding fin rockets can be easily seen on this SeaCobra. (courtesy Bell Helicopters Textron)

The twin engines and the chin turret armed with the three-barrel 20mm gun can be seen on these AH-1Js. (courtesy Bell Helicopters Textron)

transports, it could fly ahead to secure the landing area and then loiter overhead, watching over the transports while they unloaded.

But these HueyCobras were designed for the Army and the Marines still needed special features for its unique brand of operations. The AH-1G had no rotor brake, an item so necessary for shipboard operation. The Marines also wanted even more firepower than was available with the turret-mounted 7.62mm minigun installation. They needed Navy-type electronics and communications gear. Most

A pair of SeaCobras on a training mission over Camp Lejeune, North Carolina. (courtesy U.S. Marine Corps)

This head-on shot of a SeaCobra shows how narrow the attack version of the Huey really is. (courtesy U.S. Navy)

importantly, the Marines wanted twin engines. Twin engines would improve crew safety, increase reliability and ability to complete a mission, and provide growth potential for the Marines to add new weapons in the future. Twin engines were especially important for

The SeaCobra, like the HueyCobra, can carry a rather impressive array of weapons and ordnance. Of course, all the weapons shown here could not be carried at the same time. (courtesy Bell Helicopters Textron)

Two twin-engined helicopters in the Marine Corps inventory. Below, the UH-1N, and above it the AH-1J SeaCobra. (courtesy Bell Helicopters Textron)

operation over the water, where the loss of an engine on a single-engine helicopter meant sure disaster for the aircraft and often the crew.

After the success of attack helicopters during the 1968 Tet offensive, where Army AH-1Gs were a major factor in blunting the

A well-used SeaCobra landing on an amphibious transport. (courtesy U.S. Navy)

A SeaCobra and a UH-1N operating from the flight deck of a ship at sea. (courtesy Bell Helicopters Textron)

Viet Cong attack, Congress granted the Marines' request to purchase a more suitable attack helicopter. This was the interim AH-1J design. It was to have Navy-type electronics, a rotor brake, and a 20mm gun in the chin turret. But it still had a single engine. However, events in Vietnam brought about a twin-engine Marine version of the HueyCobra before the interim AH-1J went into

Another SeaCobra being readied for a mission on the deck of the amphibious transport dock USS Shreveport. (courtesy U.S. Navy)

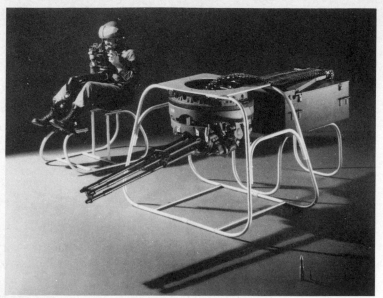

The 20mm cannon. (courtesy General Electric)

production. The Marine Corps had to replace a number of UH-1Es that it had lost in combat, as well as add to its helicopter strength in SEA, so it made sense for them to buy what they really needed, a twin-engine attack helicopter.

In October 1969, Bell displayed the twin-engined AH-1J that the Marine Corps would eventually procure. This was the Sea-Cobra, exactly the aircraft the Marines wanted. The powerplant for the SeaCobra was the Pratt and Whitney T400-CP-400, a military version of the company's PT6T-3 Turbo Twin Pac, twin-turboshaft engine, which produced a total of 1800 horsepower. The good news was that the engine was developed for the Bell Model 212, a twin-engined version of the Iroquois. This same engine would be used by the UH-1N and the Canadian Armed Forces CUH-1N. Thus, the USMC would not have to fund the engine development. The bad news was that the engine was built in Canada, going against both the U.S. government's and the aerospace industry's desire to "buy American." However, when it was found that the Canadian engine was the only one already flight-tested and in production, it was approved.

Outside of the accommodations for the twin engines and having a gross weight of 500 pounds more, the SeaCobra was almost identical to the AH-1Gs, including the same rotor head and rotor

A Marine AH-1T equipped with TOW missiles. (courtesy Bell Helicopters Textron)

A AH-1T equipped with Sidewinder air-to-air missiles. (courtesy U.S. Navy)

head system. Of course, internally and weapons-wise they were quite different. The avionics and weapon management systems were Navy and Marine Corps, rather than Army.

The SeaCobra was quite a potent machine. When fully loaded it could carry up to 2400 pounds of weapons and ammunition. Typical armament consisted of one M197 three-barrel 20mm cannon in the turret under the nose loaded with 750 rounds of ammunition. The four pylons on the stub wings could carry such weapons as an XM18E1 minigun pod, seven-tube LAU-68 2.75-inch rocket pod, the LAU-61 19-tube version, or the CBU/B Fuel-Air Explosive Bomb Cluster. Even fully loaded, it could cruise at 146 knots (166 mph), dive at 190 knots (217 mph), and had a range of 335 nautical miles (382 miles). Maximum fuel capacity was 262 gallons. Even with one engine out it cold still fly at a 2000-foot altitude carrying its maximum weight—exactly what the Corps wanted for over-the-water operation.

The first SeaCobras saw combat in early 1971, when four test AH-1Js were evaluated under real life conditions in Vietnam. The results of this evaluation were as might have been expected. The AH-1J had significantly greater effectiveness compared to the AH-1G. By June of 1971, SeaCobras were in regular use by Marine pilots. The Marine Corps purchased 67 twin-engined AH-1Js between 1970 and 1975. There were actually two more, but these were converted to the prototypes for the AH-1T, which we will discuss in a bit. The U.S. involvement in Southeast Asia was winding down before the marines had a chance to fully try out the potential of the SeaCobra in combat, however.

Like the Army, the Marines Corps saw the armor threat of the future, and they also liked the idea of having TOW-equipped Sea-Cobras comparable to the Army's AH-1Qs. Thus, the AH-1T was born. The AH-1T is basically a AH-1J with a number of significant changes. Incidentally, at the same time Bell developed its Model 309 KingCobra around Army needs, it also built an Improved SeaCobra prototype. The Improved SeaCobra used the same dynamic components as the KingCobra, such as the 48-foot diameter, 33-inch chord rotor blade, the beefed-up transmission, and the improved tail rotor, which provided for sideward flight at speeds up to 50 knots (57 mph). The Improved SeaCobra, however, was powered by twin engines, a Pratt and Whitney T400 Twin Pac, now rated at 1970 horsepower. Some of the technology developed in the Improved SeaCobra would find its way onto the AH-1T. The Improved SeaCobra was based on the last two AH-1Js made.

Getting back to the changes made for the AH-1T: First of all, the tail boom was extended some 31 inches and redesigned to include a ventral tail. This was needed to compensate for a shift in the AH-1T's center of gravity, caused when it was loaded down with all the infrared suppression, detection, jamming, and countermeasures equipment needed for the anti-armor mission. A

Another view of a Sidewinder-equipped AH-1T. (courtesy U.S. Navy)

Test firing of a Hellfire fire-and-forget missile. (courtesy Rockwell International)

12-inch extension was added behind the cockpit for future growth potential without affecting the aircraft's center of gravity. Since the AH-1T grew in gross weight from 10,000 to 14,000 pounds, more powerful engines were needed. Thus, the AH-1T is powered by twin Pratt & Whitney T400-WV-402 engines rated at 1970 horsepower. To handle the added power, the transmission was beefed up to handle 1970 horsepower (versus 1250 in the AH-1J). The rotor system was also redesigned with a 48-foot diameter 33-inch chord blades, and the dynamics from the Bell Model 214 helicopter. Both the rotor system and the engines had been developed for an Iranian version of the AH-1J.

Besides the added weight capability, this means the AH-1T can carry almost three times as much fuel and armament, and it has significantly better performance, especially at altitude. In addition to the capability of carrying four TOW tubes on the stub wing pylons, the AH-1T can carry a variety of conventional weapons, such as the standard 20mm chin gun turret and the mix of pylon-mounted weapons used with the earlier J version.

The AH-1T first flew in late spring 1976 and the Marines got their first AH-1T in the fall of 1977. While not initially TOW-equipped, of the 57 AH-1Ts built, 51 have been modified to handle the TOW.

SeaCobras for the Future

The SeaCobras were designed with considerable growth potential built in. Bell and the USMC has new versions of the SeaCobra on the drawing boards, in development, and in production.

For example, the USMC has contracted with Bell to integrate the Hellfire missile and night vision cockpit into the earlier AH-1J SeaCobras. Unlike the TOW missile, where the crew must guide the missile to the target and thus remain exposed to enemy fire, Hellfire is a "fire and forget" anti-armor missile. Hellfire is laser-guided, meaning that the target is illuminated by a laser beam and the Hellfire rides the beam to target. While the launching aircraft can illuminate the target with a laser designator, so can other sources such as a scout helicopter, a fighter aircraft, an unmanned remotely piloted vehicle, or even a foot soldier hiding behind a rock. The Hellfire launcher can pop up for only a couple of seconds to get the Hellfire off, then drop back down under protective cover—or even fire the missile from a concealed position without any exposure.

The USMC, recognizing the need for additional power in the SeaCobra, has decided to buy some 44 AH-1+ SuperCobras. The additional power comes from twin General Electric T700-GE-401

The Marine Corps' new SuperCobra attack helicopter. (courtesy General Electric)

turboshaft engines with a combined output of in excess of 3200 horsepower. The program is an outgrowth of a 1980 program in which Bell successfully tested a GE T700-GE-700 engine in an AH-1T it borrowed from the Marine Corps. The first SuperCobra equipped with the T700-GE-401 flew in the fall of 1983.

What does all this additional power in the AH-1T+ mean? Well, the Supercobra could carry eight Hellfire missiles, 750 rounds of 20mm ammunition for its chin turret gun, and two AIM-9 Sidewinder missiles on a typical mission. The Sidewinder, an *air-to-air* missile, adds a new dimension to the AH-1T's capability. It can now defend itself against enemy aircraft. The Sidewinders would be carried on top of the stub wings near the wing tip. Other ordnance that could be carried by the AH-1+ include the seven- and 19-tube 2.75-inch rocket launchers, a 20mm wing-mounted gun pod, Zuni rockets, CBU-55 fuel-air explosives, and MK 81/MK 82 bombs. The SuperCobra can cruise at 144 knots (164 mph), dive at 170 knots (194 mph), and without ordnance attached can travel at 162 knots (185 mph) in a high-speed dash lasting up to a half hour. Its range is on the order of 330 nautical miles (587 miles) and, when equipped with four auxiliary fuel tanks, it has a ferry range of almost 780 nautical miles (888 miles).

Not only does the Marine Corps plan to have new SuperCobras, it also plans to uprate its current AH-1T with the more powerful GE engines. About 40 of the AH-1Ts will be retrofitted with the T700-GE-401 and designated the AH-1T/700.

While the Marine Corps Hueys and SeaCobras number in the hundreds—compared to the Army's Hueys and HueyCobras, which have been procured by the thousands—they nevertheless are a very important part of the USMC's "air force."

Chapter 6

U.S. Air Force Hueys

When you think of the United States Air Force, hot fighters, heavy bombers, and large transports usually come to mind. However, the USAF operates a relatively large fleet of helicopters for search and rescue, supporting the Intercontinental Ballistic Missile program, transporting VIPs, and a variety of "ash and trash" type duties. For the most part, USAF helicopters have been adapted from those developed for the other services, with modifications made to meet special Air Force needs.

UH-1F

The USAF was the third service to have a Huey adapted specifically to meet its needs. This was the UH-1F. While based on the Bell Model 204 series—basically the same airframe as the UH-1B—an entirely new engine was installed. The engine was the General Electric T58-GE-3 of 1270 horsepower. The Air Force specified the GE engines mainly due to logistics implications. Various configurations of the engine were already being used by such USAF helicopters as the Sikorsky CH-3 and HH-3 and Boeing Vertol CH-46. This meant less training required for maintenance crews, and nearly the same parts inventory and engine overhaul facilities could be used.

The first F model flew in February 1964, about eight months after Bell was chosen to supply a new medium helicopter for the

While using the Model 204 fuselage, the Air Force's UH-1F was powered by a General Electric turboshaft engine. (courtesy Bell Helicopters Textron)

A USAF UH-1F in camouflage paint. (courtesy USAF)

Air Force. Originally it was designated XH-48A under Air Force terminology, but this was soon changed to the UH-1F. The Air Force eventually received 120 UH-1Fs plus another 26 TH-1Fs. The latter were essentially the same as the UH-1F except that their cockpits were configured for instrument flight training. The primary reason the USAF purchased the UH-1F was for supporting the ballistic missile force in the midwestern part of the country. For strategic reasons, missile silos are dispersed over a wide area

HH-1Hs perform an important job in searching for and rescuing downed pilots. (courtesy USAF)

The twin-engine UH-1N was developed as the CU-1N for the Canadian armed forces. (courtesy Canadian forces)

and the fastest way to transport crews is by helicopter. The UH-1F was also used as a security escort in the sky for missile convoys transporting ICBMs to and from silos.

Other UH-1Fs were assigned to the Aerospace Rescue and Recovery Service (ARRS), part of the Military Airlift Command,

Some 20 UH-1Fs were converted to UH-1Ps and used on classified missions by the USAF. (courtesy USAF)

A pair of UH-1Ns flying in formation. (courtesy Bell Helicopter Textron)

for search and rescue work in the local area of key Air Force bases. (One UH-1F assigned to the ARRS was the first USAF helicopter to pass the 10,000 hour flying mark.) Some of the UH-1Fs saw action in Vietnam, where, like their counterparts from the Army, Navy, and Marines, they had miniguns mounted in their doors. The USAF Hueys traded their characteristic blue and white paint jobs for a camouflage scheme. One of the UH-1F's key missions in SEA was search and rescue, often under heavy enemy fire. A more mundane job was the transportation of supplies and people.

The USAF does not talk much about one of the missions assigned to the Huey. About 20 F models were converted to UH-1P versions by installing classified equipment and assigned a psycho-

Several of the USAF's VH-1Ns are used to transport important government executives around the nation's capital. (courtesy USAF)

logical warfare mission. These special Huey's were assigned to the Air Force's 1st Special Operation Wing, located at Hurlburt Field in Florida. Some saw duty in Vietnam in the late 1960s.

The easiest way to distinguish a UH-1F or UH-1P is by looking at the engine installation. Because the T-58 engine has its driveshaft running towards the rear—versus running forwards, as in the Lycoming engines used in the other Hueys—the GE engine had to be installed backwards to match up with the Huey's transmission and rotor drive. Thus, the engine's exhaust was blanked off at the rear with a domelike housing and a new exhaust was installed on the right side. While the UH-1F has the same internal cargo capacity—140 cubic feet—it does have a 30-cubic-foot baggage compartment in the tail boom. That comes about because it uses the same tail boom as the Bell 205 series of helicopters, which includes the UH-1D. The UH-1F can lift 4000 pounds externally, but has a maximum gross weight capability of 9000 pounds, 500 pounds more than the UH-1B. For missile site transportation duties and other people-carrying jobs, the UH-1F is configured to carry 10 passengers plus the pilot. However, a copilot usually takes up the left seat. For medevac, three litters can be accommodated.

HH-1H

In November 1970, the USAF placed an order for 30 HH-1Hs, these being essentially identical to the UH-1H, including the 1400-horsepower Lycoming powerplant. As the designation HH implies, the HH-1Hs were mainly assigned to duties involving search and rescue of aircrews involved in accidents within the local area of airfields. They were usually kept on a ready alert status in the event they would be needed quickly. The HH-1H is fitted with a hoist for rescue work, which was not the case for the UH-1F. However, some of the TH-1Fs were equipped with hoists that were used in rescue training.

UH-1N

While the USAF, USMC, U.S. Navy, U.S. Army, Canada, and several other foreign nations purchased the UH-1N, the USAF was the first U.S. military service to take delivery of the UH-1N, when it received the first of 79 in October 1970. This was followed by an initial delivery of 40 to the Navy and 22 to the Marine Corps, followed by a substantially larger number later.

The UH-1N marked a major departure for the Huey, for the UH-1N is powered by a twin turboshaft engine. Bell's interest in a twin-engined Huey started with the Model 208 Twin Delta, a

A USAF VH-1N being prepared for a VIP transport mission. (courtesy USAF)

A USAF UH-1N on display at an airshow in Germany. (courtesy USAF)

UH-1D fitted with twin Continental T72-T-2 turboshaft engines. When mated together with a common gearbox connected to a single output shaft to the rotor, they formed the XT67-T-1, producing over 1200 horsepower. The experimental Model 208 program was initiated in 1964 in response to commercial users—primarily offshore petroleum interests—who liked the size of the larger Model 205 series of Hueys but wanted the extra margin of safety offered by twin engines for over-the-water flight. The Model 208 first flew in April 1965. The Twin Delta concept grew into the Model 212 Twin 212, probably Bell's most successful Huey-based commercial helicopter.

The credit for initiating the Model 212 can be given to the Canadians, who, in May 1968, approved funding for developing a twin-engined Huey for the Canadian Armed Forces. While the Model 212 used the Model 205 airframe, the engines were Canadian products—900-horsepower PT6s made by Pratt and Whitney of Canada. The engines were combined into one unit called the PT6T-3 Turbo Twin Pac for a total of 1800 horsepower. The military designation for this engine is the T400-CP-400. This is the same unit that would be used to power the Marine Corps' SeaCobra. And, just as with the SeaCobras, the Canadian-built engines would run up against "buy American" policies when U.S. forces wanted a version of the Model 212, but this was soon overcome when no other comparable product became available. The Canadians received the first of their 50 twin-engined Hueys in May 1971, designating them the CUH-1N, but later changing this to the CH-135. Besides delivery to U.S. armed services, military versions of the Model 212 were sold to air forces in such diverse parts of the world as Argentina and Bangladesh.

Outside of the twin engines, the specifications, dimensions, and even performance of the 1800-horsepower UH-1N are very similar to those of the 1400-horsepower HH-1Hs used by the USAF for similar missions. The big difference is in engine-out capability. The UH-1N can fly at full maximum gross weight at approximately 8000 feet of altitude on only one engine, whereas the HH-1H cannot even fly on one engine.

The U.S. Air Force put the twin Huey to work as a rescue helicopter. The UH-1N came equipped with a hoist for rescue work. Others, designated VH-1N, are used for transporting VIPs (principally around the Washington area) as part of the Air Force's 89th Military Airlift Wing, the group responsible for carrying the President on Air Force One. Some of the UH-1Hs were assigned to the Special Operations Wing at Hurlburt Field in Florida for use in the Air Force's counterinsurgency and antiterrorist activities. When armed for work in hostile territory, the Air Force UH-1N carries such weapons as two General Electric 7.62mm miniguns or two 40mm grenade launchers, and a couple of seven-tube 2.75-inch rocket pods.

Chapter 7

U.S. Navy Hueys

Even though the U.S. Navy did the procuring of Hueys for the Marine Corps, the Navy was the last of the U.S. military services to use the Huey, and it got into Huey operations in something of a backdoor manner.

Game Warden

In 1966, the U.S. Navy was assigned the task of patrolling the waterways of the Mekong Delta region of South Vietnam using Task Force 116, better known as "Game Warden." The Mekong Delta, where some 60 percent of the South Vietnamese population live on 20 percent of the land, is considered to be the world's most productive rice-producing area. At the peak of the war it was being overrun by the Viet Cong and it became the Navy's assignment to control the waterways and restrict Viet Cong movement in the region. This region of Vietnam is crisscrossed with rivers, streams, dikes, canals, and rice paddies. Even in the dry season, travel by land vehicles—especially tanks and armored personnel carriers— was next to impossible. Thus, the patrol job had to be accomplished by water-based craft. The Game Warden operation was conducted using a variety of small water craft, the most popular being PBRs (Patrol Boat, River). The PBRs were shallow draft boats propelled by General Motors 220-horsepower diesel truck engines, which drove water-jet propulsion systems built by Jacuzzi. The PBRs were

UH-1Bs escort a Patrol Air Cushion Vehicle (PACV) during Operation MOC HOA in Vietnam in 1966. (courtesy U.S. Navy)

capable of speeds of up to 30 knots (34 mph), and were typically armed with twin .50-caliber machine guns in front and a single gun in the rear. Amidship was mounted an M60 7.62mm machine gun and a Mark 18 40mm grenade launcher. The crew also had a variety of small arms they could use when they wanted to throw everything they had at the Viet Cong.

Among the interesting craft used in the operations in the Mekong Delta—at least on an experimental basis—were the PACVs or Patrol Air Cushion Vehicles. The PACVs, riding on a cushion of air about four inches above the surface, could zoom across water, mud, or dry land at speeds of up to 60 knots (68 mph). These hovercraft, known by the troops as Pack Vees, were powered by gas turbine engines that drove both the fan that provided the air cushion as well as the rear-facing propellers that propelled the craft forward. The PACVs were typically armed with .50-caliber machine guns, 40mm grenade launchers, and a variety of small arms. While they were very successful in the Mekong Delta, they were expensive to operate; by 1969 the Navy had retired them from action. The U.S. Army operated similar hovercraft, and they were another weapon system used in Vietnam that bore the Bell trademark.

From the start of the planning for the Game Warden opera-

A Patrol Air Cushion Vehicle (PACV) on patrol somewhere in Vietnam. (courtesy U.S. Navy)

As if the PACV were not fearsome enough to the Vietnamese with their noise and water spray, their crews painted sharks' teeth on the front to add to the effect. (courtesy U.S. Navy)

A Seawolf UH-1B leaving the helicopter pad at the unit's home base at the Ving Long Airfield. (courtesy U.S. Navy)

Maintenance crews of the Navy's HA(L)-3 Squadron prepare the unit's Hueys for another mission. (courtesy U.S. Navy)

tion, the Navy realized that armed helicopters would have to play an important role. Unfortunately, at that time the Navy did not have any helicopter gunships of its own, for it was not yet a Huey operator and its ship-based helicopters were needed for other vital jobs such as search and rescue and antisubmarine warfare. Besides, they were too large and expensive to be used to escort water patrol craft on their daily missions. Thus the Navy had to turn to the most ex-

One of the Seawolves' gunships fires a 2.75-inch rocket at an enemy position in the Mekong Delta. (courtesy U.S. Navy)

A Seawolf pilot's view of the war in Vietnam. (courtesy U.S. Navy)

perienced user of helicopter gunships, the U.S. Army.

Initially, U.S. Army UH-1Bs and Army crews were used to support PBR operations, but by the end of 1966 the Navy was operating eight UH-1B borrowed from the Army. By the fall of 1967, the Navy strength of UH-1Bs had grown to 22 and were operating as Helicopter Attack (Light) Squadron Three (HA [L]-3), better known as the Seawolves. The Seawolves became an elite group of men with distinguished combat records in supporting the PBRs from the air. It was not uncommon for these black-bereted aviators to earn up to 25 Air Medals during their Vietnam tour. A Seawolf Huey crew comprised a pilot, copilot, and two enlisted door gunners.

Even though the Seawolves' UH-1Bs were castoff Army helicopters, they were very effective in supporting PBRs and other armed patrol craft in contact with the enemy. The Seawolves stood on 24-hour alert and could be scrambled into the air within three minutes. Usually within 15 minutes they were attacking sampans, junks, bunkers, and fleeing troops. The Seawolves worked in two-helicopter teams, a lead and a wing chopper. While one helicopter engaged the target, the other provided cover from overhead. The Seawolves' UH-1Bs were typically fitted with seven-tube 2.75-inch rocket pods and fixed 7.62mm machine (flex) guns on either side. The door gunners were equipped with either M60 or .50-caliber machine guns, the crews preferring the latter. Also carried was a variety of grenades and small arms. The door guns proved to be the most effective weapons because they could be aimed in a semi-sphere; the forward-firing rockets and flex-guns required aiming of the entire helicopter. The biggest problem with the Navy's Hueys was that there was not enough of them. Never was the Navy able to get more than 33 UH-1Bs from the Army.

UH-1L

In 1968 and 1969, the Navy ordered its own versions of the Huey, the UH-1L, TH-1L, and the HH-1K. The UH-1L and TH-1L

A Seawolf door gunner's view of the war. (courtesy U.S. Navy)

Two Navy UH-1B gunships operating from a support ship on the Bassac River. (courtesy U.S. Navy)

were powered by the T-53-L-13 1400-horsepower engine and were directly equivalent to the Army's UH-1M, an improved version of the UH-1C. The Navy purchased only eight UH-1Ls, which were used as utility transports, but did procure 45 TH-1Ls to be used as the Navy's advanced training helicopter. The 27 HH-1Ks ordered

The door gunners on the UH-1Bs used the flexible machine guns, rockets, and hand-held automatic weapons during attacks on the Viet Cong. (courtesy U.S. Navy)

When the Navy got its own version of the Huey, it was the UH-1L. This is the first UH-1L delivered to the Navy during a test flight. (courtesy U.S. Navy)

by the Navy were fitted with the 1400-horsepower engine and equipment needed for their air sea rescue role. UH-1Ls and HH-1Ks were assigned to the Seawolves in SEA. The UH-1Ls being used by a subunit of HA(L)-3 called the Sealords.

UH-1M

In 1971, the Seawolves began replacing their UH-1Bs with UH-1Ms, the M model giving superior performance with the 1400-horsepower engine and, with larger fuel tanks, greater range and ability to remain in the target area. In August 1972, the Seawolves were deactivated after five successful years of operation. Many of their helicopter assets had been turned over to the South Vietnamese as part of the Vietnamization of the war effort. The Navy, both the regular and reserve forces, are still using a mix of UH-1Ls, TH-1Ls, and HH-1Ks.

UH-1N

The Navy also procured the twin-engined UH-1N. It was essentially identical to the Air Force UH-1N except for Navy-type electronics and gear needed for operation at sea. The Navy's

The Navy is a large user of the twin-engined UH-1N. (courtesy Bell Helicopters Textron)

This is one of the Navy's UH-1N used by Antarctic Development Squadron Six (VXE-6). (courtesy U.S. Navy)

UH-1Ns were intended mainly for air rescue work, but a few are used in supporting the Navy's Operation Deep Freeze. Annually, the Navy's Antarctic Development Squadron (VXE-6) is charged with resupplying scientists working in Antarctica and twin-engined Hueys are part of the task force. The combined Navy and Marine Corps buy of UH-1Ns surpassed the 250 mark, with a half-dozen being of the plush VH-1N VIP transport variety.

Chapter 8

Commercial Hueys

Not all Hueys were built for military and naval purposes. Many were, and still are, used for commercial applications around the world. The jobs assigned commercial Hueys range from executive transport and air taxi service to forest fire fighting and patrolling national borders.

One of the biggest uses for commercial versions of the Huey is for transporting men, equipment, and supplies to offshore oil rigs. While Bell produced several commercial versions and is in fact still producing some models in its plants in the United States, many were also produced under license in Italy and Japan.

Model 204B

The first commercial Huey produced by Bell was the Model 204B. The 204B was essentially a UH-1B with some modifications for civilian use. There were also changes through the years of production—1962 through 1967—that incorporated improvements made to the military Hueys. For example, 204Bs were built with the four-foot-longer (48 foot), 21-inch chord rotor blade and used the Lycoming T53-9 version of the 1100-horsepower turboshaft engine. Civilian avionics were naturally installed, and interiors were considerably more plush for carrying civilian passengers than for hauling military troops. The normal passenger configuration was nine, plus crew. The first 204B was delivered in the spring of 1963.

The Bell Model 204B was the first of the Hueys available to commercial users. (courtesy Bell Helicopters Textron)

The 204B could carry 140 cubic feet of cargo, internally and up to 4000 pounds could be carried from an external sling. The latter capability was an important feature, because Hueys have been used as flying cranes for everything from delivering equipment to remote construction sites to installing air conditioners on the roofs of buildings. In 1964, three 204Bs carried 1,150 tons of material and 1,500 passengers in less than two months to oil rigs in the jungles of Colombia. This was done under very demanding conditions that included sweltering humidity and temperatures up to 110 degrees F. The helicopters worked nine-hour days without even shutting down their engines to complete the herculean task. The project demonstrated the durability of turbine-powered helicopters, which could operate up to 2,000 hours between engine overhauls.

In 1964, the first 204B was introduced to forest fire fighting in Southern California. The 204B's ample capacity allowed large crews and massive amounts of firefighting equipment to be transported where needed. The 204B was also used as a platform for firefighters to parachute or rappel down ropes to quickly get as close to hot spots as possible. Hueys were also used to air-drop water and fire-retardant chemicals onto forest fires. By 1968, a special 350-gallon externally mounted helitank had been developed for this purpose.

A Bell Model 204B in action dropping fire-retarding chemicals on a forest fire. (courtesy Bell Helicopters Textron)

Before production of the Bell 204B ceased in 1967, 78 204Bs had been built—a small number compared to the vast quantities of military versions, but an important contribution to the civilian helicopter fleet.

Starting in 1961, Agusta of Italy produced its AB204B version of the 204B under license from Bell. These Italian Hueys were powered by a British-made Rolls-Royce Gnome H-1200 turboshaft engine (the British version of the T58), or by Lycoming T53s. More than 250 AB204Bs, in either civilian form or the military version, were produced by Agusta before production ended in 1974. The civilian versions were supplied to customers in Italy, Lebanon, Nor-

The Bell Model 205 had the larger fuselage used on the UH-1D/UH-1H military Hueys. (courtesy Bell Helicopters Textron)

A Bell Model 205 being used to erect electrical power transmission line in a remote area. (courtesy Bell Helicopters Textron)

way, Sweden, and Switzerland. In Japan, Fuji also built the 204B under license from Bell.

Model 205A-1

The Model 205A-1, introduced in 1967, is the commercial version of the long-fuselage UH-1H. Like the UH-1H, this model is powered by a 1400-horsepower Lycoming T53-L-13B turboshaft engine and uses 48-foot, 21-inch chord rotor blades and a standard rotor head. With seating for 15, it is especially suited for air taxi and offshore personnel transport. Its total cargo space is almost double that of the smaller 204B, being rated at 248 cubic feet including the baggage compartment in the tail boom. As an air ambulance, the 205A-1 can carry up to six litters plus two medical attendants; as an aerial crane, loads as heavy as 5000 pounds can be handled from an external sling.

Being a civilian aircraft, the 205A-1 comes equipped with such items as civilian avionics, soundproof interior headliner, and retractable passenger boarding steps as standard equipment. Many 205A-1s were equipped with such options as dual controls, cus-

The twin-engined Model 212 is especially popular with operators who must fly over open waters. (courtesy Bell Helicopters Textron)

The Model 212 is one of the most popular helicopters in the offshore petroleum industry. (courtesy Bell Helicopters Textron)

tomized interiors, high-output interior heaters, auxiliary fuel tanks, rescue hoists, rotor brakes, float landing gear, and an external cargo suspension system. Firefighting versions of the 205A-1 were able to carry 450-gallon helitanks.

Agusta in Italy also produced versions of the Model 205. The AB205A was the military version that corresponded to the UH-1H, whereas the civilian model was designated the AB205A-1. Initial models used the 1100-horsepower T53-L-11 engine, which was subsequently superceded by the installation of the T53-L-13 power-plant. In Japan, Fuji built both military and civilian versions of the 205 under license from Bell.

Model 212

The Bell Model 212 is the commercial version of the military UH-1N twin-engined Huey. The "Twin Two-Twelve," as Bell calls it, was originally powered by the PT6T-3 Turbo Twin Pac made by Pratt and Whitney of Canada, with later models using the PT6T-38 version of the Twin Pac. Rated at 900 horsepower each, the two turbines are connected to a combining transmission with a single output shaft. The transmission is rated at 1290 horsepower for takeoff, 1135 for continuous operation, and up to 1025 for single-engine operation. The latter item has made the Twin Two-Twelve

A Bell Model 212 can lift loads of up to 5,000 pounds. (courtesy Bell Helicopters Textron)

The Bell Model 214 Biglifter earned its title because it can lift more than 7,000 pounds. (courtesy Bell Helicopters Textron)

The ST in the Model 214ST's name stands for Stretched Twin, and later, Super Transport. (courtesy Bell Helicopters Textron)

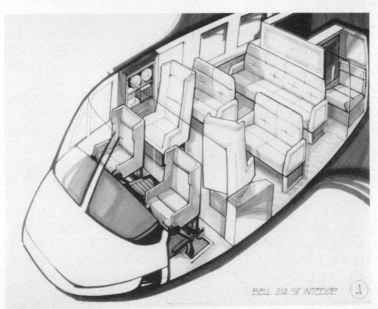

The Model 214ST's interior can be laid out in a variety of arrangements. Shown here are accommodations for 12, plus a two-man crew. (courtesy Bell Helicopter Textron)

A little fancier than a troop-carrying Huey, the interior of a VIP version of the Model 214ST. (courtesy Bell Helicopters Textron)

a very popular helicopter for offshore transportation in the petroleum industry. With auxiliary fuel tanks installed, the Model 212 can carry up to 395 gallons of fuel, giving ranges on the order of 420 nautical miles (480 miles).

Since the Model 212 uses the same airframe as the Model 205, the basic layout of the Model 212 is almost identical to the Model 205 with its 248 cubic feet of internal cargo capacity, accommodations for 14 passengers plus pilot, and ability to handle 5000 pounds of external load. Production of the 212 began in 1970.

One of the features that makes the Model 212 especially attractive to offshore operators is its optional avionics, which allow it to fly in IFR (Instrument Flight Rules) conditions. In 1977, the Twin Two-Twelve was the first helicopter certified by the FAA for single-pilot IFR operation with fixed floats. Subsequently, the 212 was certified for IFR operations by the CAA in Britain, the DOT in Canada, and the DCA in Norway. Indeed, the 212 is the most popular twin-engined helicopter in operation in the petroleum industry.

The 212 has found many other civilian applications, such as executive transport, air taxi service, border patrol, and search and rescue. The 212 was the first U.S. made helicopter to be purchased by the People's Republic of China when an order was placed in early 1979. The 10 212s flown by the Civil Aviation Administration of China are used in offshore petroleum work, as well as geophysical and forestry applications. Again, Agusta in Italy built its version of 212 under license.

Model 214B

The Bell Model 214B Biglifter is the commercial version of the Model 214A "Isfahan" designed and built for the Iranians; it went

The Model 412 is the first production Bell Helicopter to use four rotor blades. (courtesy Bell Helicopters Textron)

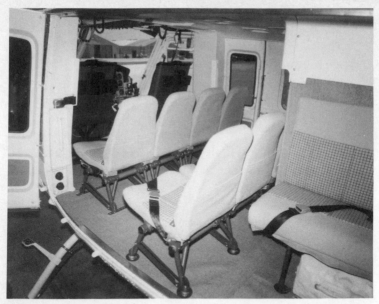

A Bell Model 412 fitted out to carry the maximum number of passengers. (courtesy Bell Helicopters Textron)

into production in 1975. Like the Isfahan, it was powered by a single Lycoming LTC 4B-8D (later designated T5508D) 2930-horsepower turboshaft engine. Other features included raked tips on both the main and tail rotors and an advanced rotor hub with elastrometric bearings.

The name Biglifter was quite appropriately chosen. The 214B is able to carry 4000 pounds of cargo internally, or up to 8000 pounds from an external sling. For dispersing chemicals in agricultural work or in firefighting, tanks of up to 800 gallons capacity can be installed. Since the 214B is also built with the Model 205 fuselage, the internal volume is essentially the same as the Model 212, as are the accommodations for 15 people including the pilot. However, the 214B's airframe was beefed up to handle the additional power and load-carrying capacity. A Model 214B-1 was also built; it differs from the Model 214B only in that its maximum gross weight is limited to 12,500-pounds (compared to the Model 214B's 13,800-pounds) in order to meet certain FAA regulations for IFR flight. The Model 214 was built by Agusta as the AB214A.

Just one example of the Biglifter's ability to take on large jobs is the one that was used in building a ski lift in Colorado. A single 214B was able to install 11 chairlift towers in a mere 37 minutes.

Doing the same work from the ground would have taken several crews at least a couple of days—and building roads would have been required to complete the job.

Model 214ST

For the Model 214ST, Bell stretched the basic Model 205 fuselage so that 18 passengers (plus pilot and copilot) could be accommodated. Interior capacity was not up to 316 cubic feet with the seats removed and there was an additional 65 cubic feet in the baggage compartment behind the cabin. Internally or externally, the 214ST is able to carry up to 8000 pounds of cargo. Initially, the ST stood for Stretched Twin, but later this was changed to Super Transport. The Model 214ST is powered by twin General Electric CT7-2A turboshaft engines rated at 1625 horsepower each. These engines offer a 30 percent reduction in fuel consumption over previous equivalent engines—a real plus in days of high fuel prices.

While the first 214ST flew in 1977, deliveries of the standard equipped, IFR-certified 214ST did not start until 1982. With the standard fuel tank capacity of 435 gallons, ranges of over 500 miles are possible and auxiliary tanks are available to increase the range even further. The 214ST is equipped with several high technology items such as an Air Data Computer, Automatic Flight Con-

A surplus UH-1B used by the U.S. Customs service in its antidrug war. (courtesy U.S. Customs Service)

Probably the only HueyCobra not operated by a military service, this one is used by the U.S. Customs Service to chase down drug smugglers. (courtesy U.S. Customs Service)

trol System, Fly-by-Wire Elevator, and main rotor blades made of composite plastic-like materials. Some of the options available include power-ejected life rafts, integral nose-mounted weather radar, and a heated bird-proof windshield. The 214ST is the first Huey available with wheels in addition to Bell's traditional landing skids.

Model 412

The Model 412 is Bell's first production helicopter to use four rotor blades instead of the company's traditional two, thus the "4" in the model designation. The additional main rotor gives improved performance along with reduced noise and vibration. The main rotor blades fold to facilitate storage. Apart from the changes in the rotor, the Model 412 is pretty much similar to the earlier Model 212, including the Pratt and Whitney Turbo Twin Pac engines. Of course, the Model 412, the first of which was delivered in 1981, does have advances over the Model 212, especially in the avionics department.

The wide variety of commercial Bell Helicopters built around the basic 204 and 205 demonstrates the versatility of the Huey's design. The fact that new Huey helicopters are still rolling off Bell assembly lines after over three decades shows how good the design was. The Huey is the rotary-wing equivalent of the venerable Douglas DC-3 airliner.

Chapter 9

International Hueys

The Huey in all its many variations is truly an international aircraft. It would be hard to find a country anywhere in the free world that does not have at least one Huey in operation somewhere in military paramilitary, police, or commercial service. Not only has Bell's most popular product been exported worldwide, it has been manufactured under license in several foreign countries—and in quite sizable quantities. Some of these foreign Hueys have even been more than just carbon copies of Hueys produced in the U.S., offering unique capabilities desired by foreign markets.

Agusta of Italy

Bell's association with Agusta, formally Costruzioni Aeronautiche Giovanni Agusta, has been a long and profitable one. As far back as 1952, Agusta was producing the Model 47 and was granted the Bell distributorship for Europe as well as countries in the Middle East and those bordering the Mediterranean Ocean. Thus it was only logical that when Bell was looking to capture the lucrative military and commercial markets with the Hueys, it should again turn to Agusta to help.

The first Agusta-built Huey flew on 10 May 1961. The AB 204B, as it was called, was a rather interesting machine. While basically a UH-1B version of the Model 204, it was powered not by a Lycoming-built engine as were the American-built Hueys, but by

The AB 205 was produced by Agusta of Italy. (courtesy Agusta)

a British-built Bristol Siddeley (later Rolls-Royce) Gnome turbine engine. Indeed, throughout the production period of the Agusta 204 series, which lasted from 1961 to 1974, the Italian-built Hueys were available with a variety of powerplants including the Gnome, the Lycoming T53, and the General Electric T-58.

A variant of the Huey rolled out of Agusta's Casina Costa plant (at the Malpensa International Airport near Milan) which had no U.S.-built counterpart. This was the AB 204 AS. The AS stood for its intended mission, anti-submarine and anti-surface vessel duties. The AB 204 AS, equipped with the 1290-horsepower T58-GE-3 engine, was typically armed with a couple of Mark 44 homing torpedoes or AS 12 antishipping missiles.

Inside the AB 204 AS's main compartment was some rather sophisticated electronics for its all-weather duties at sea. For example, there was a sonar system coupled to the aircraft's automatic stabilization system, automatic approach-to-hovering equipment, and an AN/APN 195 search radar for use in anti-submarine warfare. For anti-shipping missions, it could be equipped with the Bendix-built AN/AQS-13B search radar. The AB 204 AS could stay on station for almost two hours with a range of almost 61 nautical miles (70 miles), and had a cruising speed of slightly over 88 knots (100 mph). The range and time on station could be increased through the use of auxiliary fuel tanks. Thirty AB 204 ASs were built for the Italian Navy and two more went to the Spanish Navy.

The military version of the AB 204B was supplied to the Italian Army as well as other military and paramilitary organizations throughout the world (Austria, Ethiopia, Kuwait, Holland, Saudi Arabia, Sweden, and Turkey). The hundred or so AB-204Bs supplied to Italian military forces were used primarily for liasion, troop support, and ash and trash missions. While never developed to the level of U.S. UH-1B and UH-1C gunships, the AB 204 B supplied to military forces were fitted with a variety of weapons, usually using "home grown" installations. Agusta also built a commercial version of the AB 204B that was sold to many countries. In all, over 250 AB 204Bs of all types were built.

When Bell started manufacturing the larger capacity Model 205 series—that is, the UH-1D/UH-1H—it was only logical that Agusta be granted a license to build an equivalent model in Italy. Agusta began building the AB 205 in 1963. The original AB205s were fitted with the 1100-horsepower T53-L-13, making them equivalent to the U.S.-built UH-1D; later versions were fitted with the 1400-horsepower T53-L-13 and thus were similar to the UH-1H. The Agusta-built commercial version was the AB 205A-1, with production starting in 1969. Like the AB 204s, these larger Italian-built Hueys were placed in military and commercial service not only in Italy, but in many other countries where Agusta had distribu-

The Agusta AB 212 ASW is a lethal sub-killer which has no American counterpart. (courtesy Agusta)

This CH-135H was fitted with floats for duty in Canada's rugged north country. (courtesy Canadian Forces)

tion rights. At its peak, Agusta was producing 12 AB 205s a month.

Many of the military AB 205s were equipped with ordnance that was almost as varied as the countries that used the craft. For example, it is possible to find AB 205s equipped with Emerson 7.62mm miniguns, 2.75-inch rockets, Agusta MG-3 twin rocket systems, Rheinmetall MG-3 machine guns, or Oerlikon 80mm rockets. Countries besides Italy whose military forces were armed with the AB 205 included Iran, Kuwait, Abu Dhabi, Morocco, Saudi Arabia, Israel, Spain, Turkey, Greece, Zambia, and Oman.

In 1967, Agusta began to investigate the possibility of converting the Model 205 into a twin-engined helicopter, and two unique prototypes were built. The AB 205TA was fitted with twin Turbomeca Astazou XII engines, each producing 800 horsepower. The AB 205 Bi-Gnome used two 1250-horsepower Rolls-Royce Gnome engines. However, neither of these went into production since Agusta would be granted the license to produce the Model 212.

Agusta started delivering the AB 212 in 1971 in military and civil form. Again, Agusta produced unique anti-submarine and attack versions, the AB 212 ASW and AB 212 ASV respectively. In order to handle the large amount of gear required for these missions, the fuselage was strengthened and modified. The main trans-

A Canadian Forces CH-135 used for rescue work. (courtesy Canadian Forces)

mission cowling was also extensively revised for the radar equipment, power generator, and hydraulic equipment. However, the most distinguishing feature of these versions was the massive radome on the roof just behind the cockpit, which required beefing up of the roof. The left-hand cargo door was also modified to meet the needs of the radar operator, who sat facing rearwards in

The Canadians also use their Hueys for combat assault missions. These are CH-135 Twin Hueys. (courtesy Canadian Forces)

Bell 205s being used by the National Safety Council of Australia for aerial water bombing of fires in Australia. (courtesy NSCA)

front of his console. The door had a single window and the hinged panel in front of the sliding door was replaced by an emergency exit panel. There were other emergency doors on the right hand side. Modifications were also made to the flight controls, fuel controls, and electrical systems for the demanding job of searching for and destroying enemy submarines and surface ships, as well as search and rescue, reconnaissance, ECM early warning, and standoff missile launch. These versions of the AB 212 were designed to be quickly converted to other roles such as troop transport, administrative transport, fire support, and medevac.

The AB 212 ASW and ASV can carry an array of ordnance including the Mark 44, Mark 46, Motofide 244AS, and TP42 torpedoes; depth charges; and wire-guided, optically-tracked AS12 ASMS, France's Aerospatiale's equivalent of our TOW. For surface shipping targets, there are weapons such as the Sea Skua ASM and the Martel Mark II, a fire-and-forget missile. Using its TG-2 system, the AB 212 can guide the Otomat missile during its cruise phase, thus operating in a standoff missile guidance role. The AB 212 ASW/ASV electronics equipment is quite impressive, including a broad spectrum of communications gear from High Frequency (HF) to Ultra-High Frequency (UHF), radars for search and navigation, and sonar and magnetic anomaly detectors for finding targets. The craft are equipped with a wide variety of active and passive ECM equipment. The AS 212ASW/ASV have been put into service with both the Italian and Spanish Navies as replacements for the earlier AB 204AS helicopters. Agusta also started producing a commercial version of the AB212 in 1971.

Agusta also produced the Model 214A under license with essentially the same specifications as the 214As built for the Iranians (which are discussed below). Agusta's most recent addition is the AB 412 Griffon, which, like its U.S. counterpart the Model 412, is a four-bladed version of the twin-engined 212. However, unlike

Another view of a fire-bombing Huey in action in Australia. (courtesy NSCA)

The firefighting Hueys do not have to land to reload with water, but can suck up water through the hose shown dangling here. Belly tanks can be replenished in less than a minute. (courtesy NSCA)

U.S. 412s, which are commercial helicopters, the Griffon is a quite capable military helicopter sporting such weapons as SNORA rockets, TOW missiles, and guns up to a 25mm cannon made by Oerlikon.

Besides building the Hueys, Agusta builds a variety of other aircraft and helicopters. Indeed, Agusta is one of the world's largest helicopter manufacturers.

Dornier of Germany

Dornier AG of Oberpfaffenhofen's involvement with the Huey commenced in 1965, when West Germany decided to equip its

An Israeli Twin Huey in operation over the desert somewhere in the Middle East. (courtesy Israeli Air Force)

armed forces with the UH-1D. Originally, West Germany ordered just over 400 UH-1Ds for its Army, Navy, and Air Force, plus its police for border patrol work. However, because of economic conditions, the number of UH-1Ds built by Dornier was only 344. In addition, a couple of UH-1Ds were shipped from Bell in the U.S. and four more were assembled by Dornier using components from the U.S. Production started in 1967 and the last Dornier UH-1D was delivered in early 1971. Over 200 UH-1Ds went to the Army, some 16 were supplied to the police, and the rest went to the Luftwaffe.

In 1978, Dornier was given the job of converting some 62 AH-1Gs HueyCobras to AH-1Ss. These were aircraft already used by the U.S. Army in Europe and were sent back to their German-based units when the modifications were completed.

Fuji of Japan

Fuji Heavy Industries, of Utsonomiya, Japan, got into building Hueys when it received an order for 36 UH-1Bs in the early 1960s from the Japanese Ground Self Defense Force. In actuality, Fuji obtained a license from the Mitsui Company, who was licensed to build the civilian Model 204 in Japan. After the first 36 UH-1Bs were built, Fuji was awarded subsequent contracts to build more

137

and eventually the JGSDF would maintain slightly over 80 UH-1Bs in its inventory for several years. While the UH-1Bs used the same Lycoming engine as their American counterparts, the engines were assembled by Kawasaki from parts supplied by Lycoming and thus were designated the KT53. About 20 of these UH-1Bs were fitted out as gunships with rocket pods, and, later, TOW missiles.

The production of UH-1Bs was followed by Fuji-built versions of the UH-1H, with Kawasaki again building the 1400-horsepower KLT53-K-13B engines. The first Fuji UH-1H was delivered to the JGSDF in 1973 and production still continues today with the total number to be supplied eventually to reach over 130. The Fuji-built UH-1Hs are virtually identical to those made in the U.S. except for minor details such as a tractor-type tail rotor, and, of course, much of the electronic gear.

More recently, Fuji has begun assembling the AH-1S for the Japanese military. Again, this AH-1S is identical to the U.S.-built version, including the TOW missiles. Plans call for a total of as many as 75 AH-1S in the Japanese military inventory.

Iran's Isfahan

Prior to the revolution, Iran was America's biggest customer for military equipment. In fact, Iran was planning to buy so many Hueys that Bell designed a special version of the UH-1 specifically to meet the hot and high altitude of the Iranian environment and even planned to establish a factory in Iran to produce the craft. The result was the Bell Model 214A, known as the Isfahan, named for the location of the factory.

The Model 214 Huey Plus, which flew in the fall of 1970, was the prototype for the Isfahan. Like so many other developments in the Huey's evolution, Bell used proven components from other members of the Huey family for the Huey Plus. For starters, it used a strengthened airframe from the UH-1H. Strengthening was required because the goal was a helicopter capable of carrying up to 15 troops, 7500 pounds of cargo, and to have a gross weight of 16,000 pounds. For the Huey Plus, a 1900-horsepower Lycoming T53-L-702 engine was used. The transmission, drive, and 50-foot diameter rotor were borrowed from the KingCobra in order to improve performance as well as reduce noise and vibration.

Before production of the Model 214A began, Bell built three additional prototypes. These helicopters were powered by a 2050-horsepower T55-L-7C engine. The first of these prototype flew in March 1974.

AH-1Ss belonging to Israel are the only AH-1Ss to date that have been used in combat against real enemy armor—in this case, Syrian tanks in Lebanon. (courtesy Israeli Air Force)

When deliveries of the production Model 214As commenced in April 1975, the Model 214A was equipped with an even higher performing engine, the 2930-horsepower Lycoming LTC4B-8D. And what a performer the Isfahan was! Within a month of the first delivery to Iran, a Model 214A set some impressive performance records for its class of helicopters. The first production model climbed to a record altitude of 29,760 feet and flew in level flight at this altitude. It also climbed to 3000 meters (9843 feet), 6000 meters (19,685 feet), and 9000 meters (32,293 feet) in record times. In all, the pilot—Manouchehr Khosrowdad, head of the Imperial Iranian Army Aviation—established five world records. His copilot was Clem Bailey, a Bell test pilot. From a more practical, everyday standpoint, the Isfahan could carry 4000 pounds of internal cargo and up to 7000 pounds from an external sling. The cruising speed was 140 knots (161 mph) and the range was 248 nautical miles (283 miles).

The Isfahan was big business for Bell. The initial order of Model 214As called for nearly 300 aircraft. By 1977, production peaked at 20 per month at Bell's Texas facility. Plans were to have the Iranian Helicopter Industry build 50 more Isfahans and another 350 of the Model 214ST with twin engines and stretched fuselage. However, the overthrow of the Shah and the subsequent takeover by the revolutionary government changed all that. Bell employees in Iran were lucky to escape with their lives.

In 1976, Iran ordered 39 Model 214Cs, which were delivered in 1977 and 1978. This model was equipped for the air-sea rescue work.

Besides being built on three continents, various versions of the Huey—and even some HueyCobras—have been shipped to the far reaches of the world. Most of these are still in operation with military, paramilitary, civilian government, and commercial users. The Huey is truly an international machine.

Chapter 10

One-Offs and Record-Breakers

While various versions of the Huey and HueyCobra have been produced in vast quantities, there have been several Huey-based helicopters that have been made in very limited numbers or even in singular quantities. Most of these have been built to test new helicopter concepts or to pioneer new pieces of helicopter technology. Some of these we have already discussed as part of the evolution of the Huey and HueyCobra story, such as the XH-40, the first Huey; the Iroquis Warrior and Sioux Scout, the pathfinders for the HueyCobra; and the KingCobra, the test bed for many of the features found in the latest tank-killing HueyCobras. However, there were several other "one-off" Hueys.

Advancing Helicopter Technology

Even as capable as the helicopter is, it is still a relatively low-speed aircraft. Because of the phenomena called *retreating blade stall*, even the best-designed conventional helicopters are limited to speeds below 200 knots or so (228 mph). Retreating blade stall occurs because as the helicopter's forward speed increases, the air velocity on the portion of the rotor blade's cycle traveling backwards drops to the point where the blade stalls and there is a dramatic loss in lift. At other times, because of increased drag, the power required to travel faster may climb significantly beyond the capabilities of the powerplants installed. In either event, the helicopter is limited in the maximum forward speed which it can achieve.

For several decades the military services and the helicopter industry have been researching means to increase the maximum forward speed of the helicopter. One of the most promising means is the compound helicopter, in which supplemental engines, usually turbojets, are used to provide forward thrust for high-speed flight. One of Bell's contributions to this research was the Bell Model 533.

The Model 533 was a highly modified YUH-1B. For starters, much effort went into reducing the aerodynamic drag of the UH-1B, including streamlining the landing skids, fairing in the fuselage and rotor head assembly, and even replacing the door hinges with more streamlined ones. The traditional Bell stabilizer bar design was replaced by a variable-tilt rotor. The engine air intakes were designed to increase engine output and the tail was enlarged and reworked. Wind tunnel tests showed that drag had been reduced by over 50 percent. The improvements were confirmed in flight testing when in March 1963, the Model 533 flew over 150 knots (170 mph) in level flight, about 30 knots (34 mph) faster than a regular UH-1B could travel at full throttle. (Incidentally, the Model 533 first flew in August 1962.) Tests were also made using differing rotor designs, including three-bladed rotors and rotor heads ranging from fully gimbaled to totally rigid.

To further increase performance, two Continental J69-T-9 turbojets with 1700 pounds of thrust were mounted on pods on either side of the fuselage. With these additional engines, the Model 533 was the first rotorcraft to exceed the 200 knot (228 mph) mark, in October 1964—and it did so with some margin, actually traveling at 207 knots (236 mph). The next spring, speed shot up to 223 knots (254 mph) in a shallow dive and it was the first to attain a speed of 220 knots (250 mph) in level flight. It also could pull 2Gs and make 60-degree banking turns at 200 knots. The Model 533 was one hot machine.

Early in 1968, the compound helicopter was refitted with two Pratt & Whitney JT12A-3 turbojets, each producing 3300 pounds of thrust; these were mounted at the ends of the stub wings that were added to the UH-1B's fuselage. By 1969, this version of the Model 533 had reached speeds of 274 knots (312 mph).

In the early 1960s, other Hueys were modified to test new concepts. For example, UH-1A became the Research Helicopter 2, or RH-2, and was used to develop techniques for helping the helicopter pilot fly under poor visibility conditions by detecting objects in his path. For this testing, a high-resolution radar was mounted in a faired housing above the cockpit and this was hooked up to

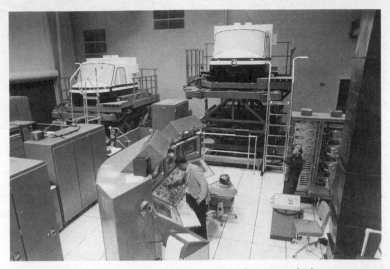

Army helicopter pilots can practice flying even under extremely dangerous conditions in these simulators. It is all done with computers. (courtesy U.S. Army)

new instrumentation and flight controls to allow the RH-2 to be flown electronically.

There was even one group of Hueys built that were never destined to get off the ground. These are the Huey simulators used in training pilots in instrument flying and for handling inflight emergencies. The simulators—built by the Link Division of the Singer Corporation, the same people who built the famous Link trainers—present a very realistic environment to the pilot. They vibrate like a Huey, tilt and rock like a real helicopter, and even reproduce the familiar sounds of the Huey including the "whup-whup" of the rotor blades. Over a hundred inflight emergencies can be simulated, and many of them—such as the loss of a tail rotor or an engine—can be duplicated without risking a helicopter and crew. If the pilot errs in handling the problem, he can learn from playing back his actions. The simulators are tied into computer consoles where operators can select the situations, monitor the pilots reactions, correct problems, and, foremost, teach proper techniques. All this can be done for a fraction of the cost of training in a real helicopter—and with *none* of the danger.

The HueyTug was another one-off prototype built by Bell that never entered production. The HueyTug was designed as a flying crane with the capability of lifting up to a three-ton load from an external sling. In order to do this, the standard UH-1C was modified with a reinforced airframe and a larger tail boom. Power came from a 2850-horsepower Lycoming T55-L-7C engine coupled to a 50-foot diameter rotor blade with a door-hinge rotor hub. The maximum takeoff gross weight of the HueyTug was about 14,000 pounds, about 6000 pounds more than the UH-1C. Even with this much added weight, the HueyTug was capable of flying at 140 knots (161 mph). Bell's traditional stabilizer bar was replaced with a stability and control augmentation system. The HueyTug was announced to the public in 1968, with the idea that modifications like those used for the HueyTug could be retrofitted to existing UH-1s; however, that was not to be.

The adaptation of the four-bladed main rotor (first used on the Model 412 commercial helicopter) to military Hueys and Huey-Cobras has lead to some interesting prototypes. For example, the Huey II was a UH-1H with a four-bladed rotor and a transmission, drivetrain, and tail rotor borrowed from the AH-1S version of the HueyCobra. With those modifications, the Huey II was able to carry 1400 pounds of cargo than the UH-1H. Adding the Model 412 main rotor system to the twin-engined UH-1N resulted in the Advanced Twin Huey, which could carry about 1000 more pounds of payload, or with the same gross weight as the UH-1N, could cruise at speeds of about 18 knots (20 mph) faster than the UH-1N. Both the Huey II and Advanced Huey used beefed-up fuselages to handle the additional load, as well as high-technology electronics.

With the addition of the Model 412 rotor to the YAH-1S version of the HueyCobra, Bell had its Model 249, an attack helicopter prototype used to try out several new ideas. Some of these included equipment that made it a night-fighter. Another version of the Model 249 was called the PAH-2 Cobra, an attack helicopter proposed to the Federal Republic of Germany and other NATO countries as a anti-tank helicopter with day and night target acquisition and engagement capability. The chin turret was deleted on the PAH-2 and in its place was installed an advanced Target Acquisition Designation System (TADS) and Pilot Night Vision System (PNVS). The PAH used the GE T700-GE-701 engine.

For the Record

Since helicopters are not normally thought of as high-performance aircraft, the flight records they have set through the years may not have been as glamorous, perhaps, as those established by high-performance fighters or other experimental aircraft. Nevertheless, helicopter records are kept by the Federation

This Model 533 compound helicopter set several records for rotary-wing aircraft. One of the Turbojet Jet engines used for high speed flight can be seen attached to the fuselage. (courtesy U.S. Army)

Aeronautique Internationale (FAI), the world body for such activities, and are aggressively sought by both rotary-wing aircraft manufacturers and operators.

Right from the start, the Huey was a record setter. A team of U.S. Army pilots that included Colonel Jack Martinelli, Major C. J. Boyle III, and Chief Warrant Officer C. V. Turvey were the first to use a Huey—in this case a HU-1A—to set rotary-wing flight records recognized by the FAI. These included both time-to-climb and speed records. For the record, the HU-1A was able to climb to 3,000 meters (9,843 ft) in 3 minutes, 29.1 seconds and to 6000 meters (19,686 ft) in 8 minutes, 7.1-seconds (the FAI uses the metric system in recording records). In a 3-kilometer (1.86-mile) speed run, the HU-1A had an average speed of 254.286 km/hr (158.04 mph). For closed circuit runs of 50, 100, and 500 kilometers (31, 62, and 310 miles), the HU-1A attained record speeds of 238.906, 228.831, and 238.906 km/hr (148.481, 142.22, and 148.481 mph), respectively.

When the U.S. Army got its larger-bodied Model 205 Huey, it again went after records with its YUH-1D prototype, this time with a team comprising Lt. Colonel Leland Wilhelm and Captains Boyce B. Buchner and W. F. Gurley. In times-to-climb it shaved minutes off the records previously held by the HU-1A, climbing to 3000 meters in 2 minutes, 17.3 seconds and to 6000 meters in 5 minutes, 47.4 seconds. The record over a 1000-kilometer (620-mile) closed circuit was set at 217 km/hr (134.9 mph). These record setting flights were made between April 13 and 20, 1962.

The UH-1D gave the Army another reason to try for world's records again with a team of Army pilots. This time the team consisted of Major John A. Johnston, Captains Michael N. Antoniou and William L. Welter, Jr., and Chief Warrant Officers Emery B. Nelson and Joseph C. Watts. The flights were made between September 16 and October 7, 1964. In the time-to-climb department, records to 3000 meters, 6000 meters, and now 9000 meters were set at 2 minutes, 9.6 seconds; 4 minutes, 35.8 seconds; and 9 minutes, 13.7 seconds, respectively. Over the 1000 kilometer closed circuit, the record-setting speed was 225 km/hr (140 mph); on the 2000-kilometer circuit, the speed was 215.626 km/hr (133.9 mph).

The UH-1D also set some long-distance records. Records for distances over a closed circuit included 1999 kilometers (1242.8 miles) and 2600.189 kilometers (1614.6 miles), and over a 2170.7-kilometer (1348.8 miles) straight-line course from Edwards AFB, California to Rogers, Arkansas.

As a final assault on records, the Army put together a team of Lt. Colonel Richard J. Kennedy, Majors B. L. Odneal, L. R. Dennis, J. K. Foster, and E. F. Sampson, and Captains R. A. Chubboy, J. F. Cromer, and D. P. Wray to make a series of record attempt flights between November 16 and December 16, 1964. Besides setting more records over distances of 3, 15, 25, 100, 500, and 1000 kilometers, at speeds of up to 289 km/hr (180.14 mph), the team went after some altitude records, including a maximum altitude of 10,713 meters (35,150 feet) without any payload.

At one time, the U.S. held 35 out of a possible 61 recognized flight records for helicopters; of these, some 27 were set with the UH-1D. Most of these were accomplished with a standard UH-1D, but with weight modifications made to meet competition rules. The bulk of the record-setting flights were made at the U. S. Army Test Activity located on Edwards AFB.

Previously in this chapter were mentioned the speed barriers that were broken by Bell's Model 533 compound helicopter. In Chapter 9 are listed the records set by the Iranian Isfahan.

Chapter 11

Replacements
for the Huey Family

As in the case for all weapons, new enemy threats, military requirements, and technology lead to new helicopter designs to replace old ones. There are replacements already in the field, with more in development that will eventually replace the Huey and Cobra and provide even more capability. However, Hueys and Huey-Cobras will probably still be used by the U.S. military well into the 21st Century. Commercial operators will be using Hueys for decades; indeed, Bell recently introduced a new version of the Huey, the 412SP, the SP standing for Special Performance. The Huey falls into that category of aircraft whose life seems endless—like the classic DC-3, still in use after more than a half century, and the B-52, still a first-line USAF bomber after three decades of service. However, it is interesting to see what the U.S. Army foresees as the replacements for the Huey and HueyCobra.

UH-60A Blackhawk

The Blackhawk is the Army's first true squad-carrying helicopter, thus performing the same role as the UH-1D and UH-1H Hueys. It is capable of carrying a full 11-man fighting unit and all their combat gear, as well as a three-man flight crew. Now the Army has the capability to deposit an entire squad onto the battlefield as an integral team ready and equipped for combat. As good as the Army's Hueys are, they do not have this ability. In the combat as-

148

The Sikorsky-built UH-60A Blackhawk is capable of carrying a fully equipped Army squad into battle. (courtesy Sikorsky Aircraft)

sault role, the UH-60A has a useful payload of almost 6000 pounds, which includes the fully equipped squad and sufficient fuel for a 211-nautical mile (241-mile) round trip. Like the Huey, the Blackhawk can be used to extract troops, resupply them, and reposition fighting teams as needed.

The Blackhawk is also used for medical evacuation, being able to carry four litters, attending medical personnel, and life-sustaining equipment. The UH-60A is also an administrative transport for the myriad of "ash and trash" missions required by the Army and can even lift up to 8000 pounds suspended from an external sling.

The UH-60A is powered by twin 1560-horsepower T700-GE-700 gas turbine engines. While producing 10 percent more horsepower than the engines used in the UH-1H, they are 40 percent lighter, weighing slightly more than 400 pounds each. Most importantly, the T700-GE-700 uses 20 to 30 percent less fuel than its predecessors.

As a rough comparison of the capability of the UH-60A versus the UH-1H, a combat lift company with 15 Blackhawks can provide the same lift capability as 23 UH-1Hs. Additionally, the cost of operating a UH-60A is approximately the same as for one Huey, even though the Blackhawk is more complex.

While primarily a troop transport, the Blackhawk does carry some armament for defensive and fire suppression purposes; two M60 machine guns and a total of 1100 rounds of ammunition are typical on assault missions. Some versions of the Blackhawk can come more heavily armed, with up to sixteen Hellfire missiles for anti-armor missions.

AH-64 APACHE

The AH-64 represents a significant improvement over even the quite capable AH-1S HueyCobra equipped with TOW missiles. First of all, the Apache is designed to operate under more demanding altitude, weather, and temperature conditions. It is also more reliable and more survivable against projected enemy threats. It is easier to maintain, and most important, it is armed with more capable weapons.

For starters, the Apache uses twin T700-GE-701 engines, essentially the same engine as used in the Blackhawk, greatly reducing the Army's logistics problem both at home and in the field. Also, twin-engine capability in both the Blackhawk and Apache give an added margin of safety, since both can make it back to safe territory on a single engine. While the Apache's cruise and maximum

The AH-64A Apache is a fearsome attack helicopter. (courtesy McDonnell Douglas Helicopters)

The YAH-63 was Bell Helicopter's entry into the Advanced Attack Helicopter competition. (courtesy U.S. Army)

Just one of the many concepts proposed for the LHX program. This scout and attack version, or SCAT, from Hughes Helicopters, would work with a noise-reducing tail rotor. (courtesy McDonnell Douglas Helicopter Company.

speed depend on the load it is carrying and the environment in which it is flying, under ideal conditions it can reach a maximum speed of 164 knots (187 mph).

With its four wing stations it can carry over 6000 pounds of ordnance, including up to 16 Hellfires, 76 2.75-inch FFAR rockets, or six Sidewinders. The weapon's pylons can also be adapted to carry anti-ship missiles such as the Harpoon or Penguin. For going against ground troops or raking over a landing zone prior to a troop assault, the Apache has the very potent 30mm chain gun mounted in its chin turret. The chain gun can fire at a rate of 625 rounds per minute from a 1200-round magazine. The Apache is designed for rapid reloading in combat. For example, reloading 76 FFARs or 1200 rounds of chain gun ammunition takes 10 minutes and loading on 16 Hellfires takes a mere five minutes.

The Apache uses much high-technology componentry that allows it to fly and locate and destroy targets day or night and in adverse weather. For example, the Target Acquisition and Designation Sight (TADS) enables the copilot/gunner to accurately search, detect, recognize, and engage targets at significant standoff ranges. The TADS incorporates high-powered optics, a

Forward Looking Infrared (FLIR) sensor for operations at night, a high-resolution television system for daytime work, a laser tracker, and a laser target designator/rangefinder. While the TADS is primarily operated by the copilot, the pilot can use its displays. The Pilot Night Vision Sensor (PNVS) working through the Integrated Helmet and Display Sight System (IHADSS) is the pilot's primary tool for flying and maneuvering in even total darkness. The PNVS's key component is its FLIR. In simplest terms, the PVNS gets the Apache to the target while TADS locates and destroys it. As in the HueyCobras, the pilot sits behind the copilot/gunner.

The U.S. Army learned a lot about survivability in combat by using the Huey and HueyCobra in Vietnam. Thus, when both the UH-60 and AH-64 designs were started on fresh sheets of paper, survivability was a key ingredient. There are two parts to the topic of survivability: first, if at all possible, avoid detection by the enemy. Second, if detected, minimize the enemy's ability to do damage. Superior maneuverability—especially by nap-of-the-Earth flying—greatly aids both of these goals, but there is much more that can be done and was done for both the Blackhawk and Apache.

Let us take a closer look at the Apache as an example of current technology available for reducing detectability. The AH-64 incorporates a low-flicker rotor, and, like the latest AH-1Ss, flat canopy window panels to reduce the visual signature. Noise is reduced through careful design of both the main and tail rotors. Both passive suppression of the engine exhaust and active IR jam-

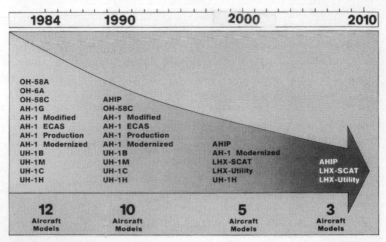

1984	1990	2000	2010
OH-58A OH-6A OH-58C AH-1G AH-1 Modified AH-1 ECAS AH-1 Production AH-1 Modernized UH-1B UH-1M UH-1C UH-1H	AHIP OH-58C AH-1 Modified AH-1 ECAS AH-1 Production AH-1 Modernized UH-1B UH-1M UH-1C UH-1H	AHIP AH-1 Modernized LHX-SCAT LHX-Utility UH-1H	AHIP LHX-SCAT LHX-Utility
12 Aircraft Models	**10** Aircraft Models	**5** Aircraft Models	**3** Aircraft Models

The Army plans on using the Huey and HueyCobra as part of its light helicopter fleet right into the 21st Century. (courtesy McDonnell Helicopter Company)

mers reduce the enemy's ability to detect, track, and destroy the Apache using its infrared signature. Special infrared paint further reduces the infrared detectability. Finally, to reduce the radar signature, there are such features as a radar jammer and chaff dispenser, as well as a sophisticated "fuzzbuster" to tell the Apache crew when a radar is beamed on them.

The Apache is essentially invulnerable to enemy small arms hits, and nearly invulnerable to projectiles up to 23mm. It also has twin engines, self-sealing fuel tanks, redundant fly-by-wire flight controls, and ballistically tolerant components that not only allow the Apache to return home safely, but in most cases even complete the mission after being hit by the enemy. The crew is protected by crew compartment armor and blast/fragment shields.

While Hughes Helicopters (now the McDonnell Douglas Helicopter Company) is building the AH-64A, Bell Helicopters Textron was the other contender for the Advanced Attack Helicopter, as the Apache program was originally called. Bell's entry in the competition was the YAH-63. While the YAH-63 was new from the ground up, the Bell YAH-63 prototype drew on the vast experience the company had gained in building the HueyCobra. Like the competitor from Hughes, the Bell entry used twin T700-GE-700 engines. However, unlike previous Bell attack helicopters, the crew positions were reversed. The reasoning was that with all the sophisticated systems for controlling the weapons, the copilot/gunner would have his eyes "buried" in his displays most of the time. Unlike the weapons used in the HueyCobras, which required visibility of the outside world, most of the new weapons could be fired "in the dark." Thus the pilot would need all the visibility he could get to perform as a defensive gunner and for flying nap-of-the-Earth at altitudes of 50 to 100 feet—and even lower. As previously mentioned, the Hughes AH-64A uses the more conventional seating arrangement.

The Light Helicopter Family

The U.S. Army is currently planning to develop a new family of helicopters to replace its huge fleet of light helicopters, which they believe will lack the ability to perform in the combat environment of the 21st Century. The Army is calling this new generation of helicopters the Light Helicopter Family, or LHX for short. There are two versions of the LHX planned. The light utility version would be used for transporting less than full squad-size combat groups as well as the myriad of jobs the term "utility" implies. The

Scout/Attack, or SCAT, version would be used for such missions as surveillance and reconnaissance, defensive suppression of ground and air threats, anti-armor, and armed escort. For these missions, the SCAT would be armed with missiles such as the Hellfire and Stinger. It would also be equipped with a turret-mounted gun and the familiar 2.75-inch rockets.

The name of the game in developing the LHX is high technology. Advanced technology will be applied not only to make the LHX highly capable of performing its missions, but also to make it more reliable, simpler to maintain, more survivable on the battlefield, and easier to fly. In line with the latter requirement, one of the goals of the program is the elimination of the need for a copilot. High technology will be required to reduce pilot workload, especially under combat conditions. Thus at least the SCAT version of LHX will probably use such advanced technologies as a Helmet Mounted Display (HMD) coupled with interactive voice controls that would allow the pilot to control aircraft functions by merely looking at the desired control and giving a voice command. The key information for flying and firing weapons would probably be projected right on the visor of the helmet so that the pilot would not have to look down at his instruments, distracting him from the world outside. Because of the sophisticated electronics available to the pilot, the LHX will require super computer power. Thus, technologies such as the Very High Speed Integrated Circuit (VHSIC) will be vital to the LHX.

Of all the new helicopter systems mentioned here, the UH-60A Blackhawk and AH-64A Apache are already in operation with regular Army units. The Blackhawk is not really all that new, the first prototype flying in 1974 and deliveries to the Army starting in 1978. Thus the thousand or so Blackhawks are already seasoned Army veterans. The Apache is somewhat newer. First flights of the Bell and Hughes prototypes occurred in 1975, and the Army got its first Apaches in 1984. Plans are to build about 675 AH-64As before production ceases in 1990.

The LHX is really an aircraft for the 21st Century. The first LHXs will not start entering the Army inventory until the mid-1990s. The LHX could represent the largest purchase of helicopters in aviation history, with as many as 5000 to 6000 LHXs envisioned. At this writing, Bell Helicopter is one of the contenders for this important helicopter program.

Appendix A:

Huey and HueyCobra Variants

Through the years, there have been numerous versions of the Huey, HueyCobra, their civilian counterparts, and special research helicopters. Here is a listing of all the known derivatives of the helicopters that started with the XH-40.

AB204B: Italian-built version of the Model 204 built under license by Agusta for both the military and civilian markets.

AB204AS: Agusta's anti-submarine and anti-surface vessel version of the AB204.

AB205: Italian-built version of the UH-1D/UH-1H produced by Agusta.

AB205A-1: Agusta's version of the commercial Model 205A-1.

AB205BG: Twin-engined Agusta prototype using two Rolls-Royce engines.

AB205TA: Twin-engined Agusta prototype using two Antazou, P&W, or Continental engines.

AB212: Agusta's version of the twin-engined Model 212. Built in both military and commercial forms.

AB212ASW/ASV: Naval version of the AB212 built by Agusta.

AB214A: Military version of the Model 214 built by Agusta.

AB412 Griffon: Agusta's version of the Model 412; however, designed for military uses.

Advanced Twin Huey: Military Huey prototype based on the Model 412 four-bladed commercial helicopter.

AH-1G: The original Army attack helicopter derived from the Huey that went into series production.

AH-1J: The modified version of the AH-1G having, among other things, twin engines. Used by the USMC and known as the SeaCobra.

AH-1Q: Anti-armor version of the AH-1G HueyCobra with capability to launch the TOW missile.

AH-1R: Army's uprated version of AH-1G with a more powerful engine but without the ability to launch the TOW missile.

AH-1S: Advanced version of the HueyCobra with an uprated engine and capability of launching the TOW missile for anti-armor use.

AH-1T: Advanced version of the AH-1J SeaCobra for the USMC with uprated engines and TOW missile launching capability.

AH-1T+: Prototype attack helicopter designed for the USMC with twin GE engines for improved performance.

CH-118: Canadian redesignation for the CUH-1H.

CH-135: Canadian redesignation for the CUH-1N.

CUH-1H: Canadian designation for the UH-1H. Later redesignated CH-118.

CUH-1N: Canadian designation for the UH-1N. Later redesignated CH-135.

D255: Bell designation for the Iroquois Warrior, mockup for an attack helicopter.

EH-1H: Electronic warfare helicopter for U.S. Army Security Agency's Project Quick Fix.

Fuji Model 204B: Version of the Model 204 built by Fuji in Japan.

HH-1H: USAF search and rescue helicopter based on the UH-1H.

HH-1K: U.S. Navy search and rescue helicopter based on the UH-1L.

HU-1: U.S. Army preproduction designation for the Huey.

HU-1A: First production Huey. Later designation changed to UH-1A.

HU-1B: Second Huey production model for the U.S. Army. Later redesignated the UH-1B.

JUH-1: Huey used for the Army's Standoff Target Acquisition System Program.

Model 204: Bell's generic designation for all short fuselage Hueys starting with the XH-40.

Model 204B: Commercial and military export version of the UH-1B.

Model 205: Bell's generic designation for all longer fuselage Hueys starting with the UH-1D.

Model 205A-1: Commercial version of the Model 205.

Model 207: Bell designation for the Sioux Scout, forerunner of the HueyCobra.

Model 208: Twin-engine precursor for the UH-1N. Also known as the Twin Delta.

Model 209: Bell's generic designation for the HueyCobra and SeaCobra.

Model 212: Bell's generic designation for the twin-engined Huey.

Model 214 Huey Plus: Prototype for the Model 214ST.

Model 214A: Helicopter built for the Iranians and called the Isfahan.

Model 214C: Search and rescue version of the Model 214A, also built for Iran.

Model 214B Biglifter: Commercial version of the Model 214A.

Model 214ST: Twin-engined, stretched version of the Huey for commercial applications. Also called the Super Transport.

Model 249: YAH-1S modified by incorporating the four-bladed rotor system from the Model 412. Also known as the Cobra/TOW 2.

Model 309: Bell's designation for Bell's KingCobra single and dual-engine advanced attack helicopter designs.

Model 412: Commercial version of the Huey that uses a four-bladed rotor. Otherwise, essentially the same as the Model 212.

Model 412SP: Improved version of the Model 412.

Model 533: Bell's designation for the YUH-1B experimental compound helicopter.

NUH-1B: Research helicopter based on the UH-1B.

RH-2: Research helicopter based on the UH-1A.

TH-1A: Training version of the UH-1A for the U.S. Army.

TH-1F: Training version of the UH-1F for the USAF.

TH-1G: Trainer version of the AH-1G.

TH-1L: Training version of the UH-1E for the U.S. Navy.

Twin Two-Twelve: Commercial version of the Model 212 twin-engined Huey.

UH-1A: First production Huey. Based on the Model 204.

UH-1B: Second U.S. Army Huey version. Based on Model 204.

UH-1C: Third U.S. Army Huey version. Based on Model 204. Used as a gunship and utility transport.

UH-1D: Army troop transport based on the longer fuselage Model 205.

UH-1E: USMC equivalent of the UH-1B.

UH-1F: USAF utility transport based on the Model 204 but powered by General Electric engines.

UH-1H: U.S. Army utility helicopter similar to the UH-1D but with uprated engines.

UH-1L: U.S. Navy utility transport based on the Model 204.

UH-1M: Uprated version of the UH-1C with more powerful engines. Also, special test Hueys used to evaluate new systems in Vietnam.

UH-1N: Twin-engined version of the Huey used by the U.S. Army, USAF, USMC, and U.S. Navy.

UH-1P: USAF psychological warfare helicopter based on the UH-1F.

UH-1V: U.S. Army medical evacuation helicopter.

VH-1N: VIP transport versions of the twin-engined UH-1N used by the USAF, USMC, and U.S. Navy.

XH-40: Original Huey experimental prototype.

XH-48A: Original designation for the USAF UH-1F.

XMH: Compound experimental helicopter built by Fuji in Japan.

XHU-1: Redesignation of the XH-40.

YAH-1Q: Service evaluation prototype for the AH-1Q.

YAH-1R: Service evaluation prototype for the AH-1R.

YAH-1S: Service evaluation prototype for the AH-1S.

YH-40: Designation for the Huey prototypes used in early evaluations.

YHU-1D: Original designation for the UH-1D prototype.

YUH-1D: Prototype for the UH-1D.

Appendix B

Product History

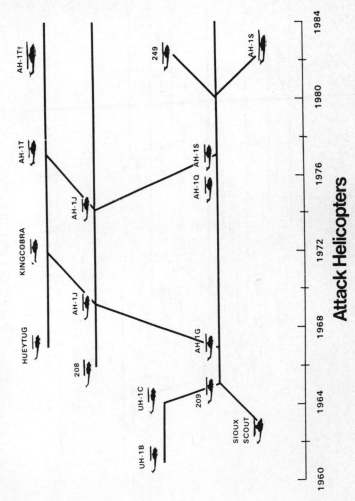

Attack Helicopters

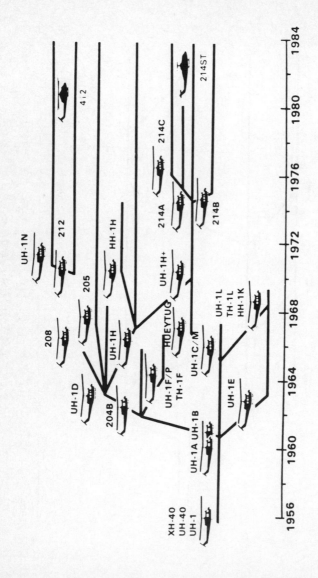

Transport Helicopters

Common Huey Armament Systems

Designation	Description
M3	2.75-inch rocket system. One 24-round rocket launcher attached to each side of Huey.
M5	40mm M75 grenade launcher turret attached to nose of Huey.
M6	7.62mm machine gun system. Two flexible M60C machine guns mounted on each side. 6000 rounds carried internally.
M16	M6 system with two 7-round 2.75-inch rocket pods added.
M21	7.62mm XM134 minigun and 2.75-inch M158 rocket system. One system attached to each side of Huey.
M22	Point target missile system attached to hardpoints on each side of helicopter.
M23	Single 7.62mm M60C machine gun installed in door on each side.
XM93	GAU-2B/A 7.62mm minigun on a USAF/GE developed pintle mount with fixed sights and dual triggers. Installed on either or both sides in doorway.
XM94	Two M129 40mm grenade launchers installed on the pintle mount used for the XM93. Can be remotely fired by pilot when fixed in a forward position.
XM165	Tactical CS canister cluster carried as an alternate to rocket pods on the M16 or M21 system.

U.S. Army Hueys at a Glance

	UH-1A	UH-1B	UH-1C	UH-1D	UH-1H	UH-1M
Model						
Missions	Instrument Trainer Troop Transport Medevac Cargo	Fire Support Troop Transport Medevac Cargo	Fire Support Troop Transport Medevac Cargo	Troop Transport Medevac Cargo	Troop Transport Medevac Cargo Command/Control	Fire Support Troop Transport Medevac Cargo
Powerplant	T53-L-1A	T53-L-5/9/11	T53-L-11	T53-L-11	T53-L-13B	T53-L-13
Horsepower	860 SHP	960/1100 SHP	1100 SHP	1100 SHP	1400 SHP	1400 SHP
Rotor						
Blade Length	44 ft	44 ft	44 ft	48 ft	48 ft	44 ft
Blade Chord	15 in	21 in	27 in	21 in	21 in	27 in
Type	Standard	Standard	540	Standard	Standard/540	540
Weights						
Max. Gross	7200 lb	8500 lb	9500 lb	9500 lb	9500 lb	9500 lb
Empty	3930 lb	4523 lb	4827 lb	4938 lb	5210 lb	5110 lb
Internal Fuel Capacity	125 gal	165 gal	242 gal	211 gal	211 gal	242 gal
Performance						
Max.Cruise(1)	68 kts	95 kts	111 kts	110 kts	110 kts	125 kts
Max.Range(1)	117 nm	193 nm	260 nm	251 nm	266 nm	288 nm
Hover Ceiling(2)						
IGE	8000 ft	8200 ft	2400 ft	5500 ft	14,200 ft	10,700 ft
OGE	6400 ft(3)	2500 ft	1900 ft(4)	3100 ft(5)	4000 ft	7700 ft(4)
Rate of Climb(1)	1349 fpm	1500 fpm	863 fpm	1080 fpm	1600 fpm	1400 fpm
Vertical R/C	460 fpm	500 fpm	400 fpm(4)	500 fpm(5)	240 fpm	550 fpm(4)

Notes: (1) Sea Level at Maximum Gross Weight, except as noted
(2) At Maximum Gross Weight   IGE = In Ground Effect, OGE Out of Ground Effect
(3) Gross Weight = 6600 lbs
(4) Gross Weight = 8500 lbs
(5) Gross Weight = 8800 lbs

U.S. Army Attack Helicopters at a Glance

	AH-1G	AH-1S Modified	AH-1S Modernized
Powerplant	T53-L-13	T53-L-703	T53-L-703
Horsepower	1400 SHP	1800 SHP	1800 SHP
Rotor			
Diameter	44 ft	44 ft	44 ft
Chord	27 in	30 in	30 ft
Type	540	540	540
Weights			
Max. Gross	9500 lb	10,000 lb	10,000 lb
Empty	5809 lb	6300 lb	6598 lb
Internal Fuel			
Capacity	268 gal	259 gal	259 gal
Performance			
Max. Cruise(1)	129 kts		134 kts
Max. Range(1)	325 nm	295 nm	290 nm
Hover Ceiling(2)			
IGE	9700 ft	12,000 ft	12,250 ft
OGE	7000 ft(3)	10,500 ft(4)	10,500 ft(4)
Rate of Climb (1)	1370 fpm		
Vertical R/C	600 fpm(3)	420 fpm	420 fpm

Notes: (1) Sea Level At Maximum Gross Weight, except as noted
(2) At Maximum Gross Weight   IGE = In Ground Effect,
                                   OGE = Out of Ground Effect
(3) Gross Weight = 8800 lb
(4) Gross Weight = 9500 lb

AH-1G Armament

M28   Dual chin-mounted gun turret with two weapons. The 7.62mm mini-gun can fire at either 1300 or 4000 rpm rates and 4000 rounds of linked ammunition can be carried in the bay behind the turret. The 40mm grenade launcher fires at 400 rpm and 300 rounds are carried. The M28 turret can be configured for (1) one minigun and one grenade launcher, (2) one or two miniguns, or (3) two grenade launchers.

XM35   20mm XM195 cannon carried on left inboard pylon with two faired ammunition boxes flush to the fuselage below the wings. Fixed in azimuth and elevation. Firing rate is 750 to 800 rpm with 1000 rounds carried. Not all AH-1Gs can carry this weapon.

M158   Rocket launcher. Holds seven 2.75-inch folding fin aerial rockets. Fixed in elevation and azimuth. Rockets can be fired individually or in ripple.

M200   Rocket launcher. Holds 19 2.75-inch folding fin aerial rockets. Fixed in elevation and azimuth. Rockets can be fired individually or in ripple.

M18   7.62mm minigun pod attached to wing pylon. Fires at a rate of 2000 or 4000 rpm. 1500 rounds carried. Fixed in elevation and azimuth.

M118   Smoke grenade dispenser

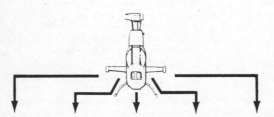

M200	M200	M28	M200	M200
M158	M200	M28	M200	M158
M200	M158	M28	M158	M200
M158/200	M18	M28	M18	M158/200
M118				M118
M118	M18	M28	M18	M118
		M28	XM35	

Armament Configurations for Modernized AH-1S

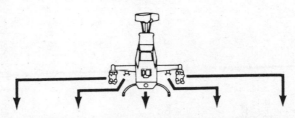

4 TOW		M197		4 TOW
4 TOW	M158	M197	M158	4 TOW
2 TOW	M200	M197	M200	2 TOW
M158	M200	M197	M200	M158

M158 - Seven 2.75 in rocket pod.
M197 - 20mm cannon.
M200 - Nineteen 2.75 in rocket pod.
TOW - Tube-launched, optically-tracked, wire-guided missile.

Note: Lightweight rocket launchers are also available—M260 with seven rockets and M261 with 19 rockets.

Armament Carried by the Modified and Modernized AH-1S

Armament Configuration	20mm M195 Cannon	40mm Grenade Launcher	7.62mm Minigun	2.75-in M151/M229 Rockets	TOW	Fuel
Modified AH-1G						
Alternate I (9,877 lb gross wt)	—	250 rds	4000 rds	—	8 rds	1684 lb
Alternate II (9,935 lb gross wt)	—	—	8000 rds	—	8 rds	1684 lb
Alternate III (10,000 lb gross wt)	—	—	4000 rds	14 rds	8 rds	1682 lb
Modernized AH-1S						
Alternate I (9,978 lb gross wt)	750 rds	—	—	—	4 rds	1684 lb
Alternate II (10,000 lb gross wt)	750 rds	—	—	14 rds	—	1489 lb
Alternate III (10,000 lb gross wt)	750 rds	—	—	—	8 rds	1370 lb

Note: The M28 turret is installed on the Modified AH-1S and early production AH-1S. The M28 can be fitted with any of these combination of weapons: (1) one 7.62mm minigun and one 40mm grenade launcher, (2) one or two 7.62mm minigun or (3) two 40mm grenade launchers.

Marine Corps Hueys and HueyCobras at a Glance

Model	UH-1E	AH-1J	AH-1T/TOW	AH-IT +
Missions	Armed Reconnaissance Troop Transport Medevac/Rescue Cargo	Armed Escort Fire Support	Anti-armor	Anti-armor Fire Support
Powerplant	T53-L-11	T400-CP-400	T400-WV-402	T700-GE-401
Number	1	2	2	2
Horsepower	1100	1800 (Total)	1970 (Total)	3250 (Total)
Rotor				
Blade Length	44 ft	44 ft	48 ft	48 ft
Blade Chord	27 in	27 in	33 in	33 in
Type	540	540	540	540
Weights				
Max. Gross	9500 lb	10,000 lb	14,000 lb	14,000 lb
Empty	5140 lb	6610 lb	8553 lb	-
Internal Fuel Capacity	242 gal	268 gal	312 gal	-
Performance				
Max. Cruise(1)	119 kts	131 kts	136 kts(5)	144 kts
Max. Range(1)	262 nm	325 nm	312 nm	329 nm
Hover Ceiling(2)				
IGE	10,150 ft	11,800 ft	5000 ft	10,000 ft
OGE	8000 ft(3)	3800 ft	800 ft	4500 ft
Rate of Climb(1)	1160 fpm	1090 fpm	-	-
Vertical R/C	545 fpm(3)	250 fpm(4)	-	-

Notes: (1) Sea Level at Maximum Gross Weight, except as noted
(2) At Maximum Gross Weight, IGE = In Ground Effect, OGE = Out of Ground Effect
(3) Gross Weight = 8500 lbs
(4) Gross Weight = 9616 lbs

169

Armament Carried by USMC SeaCobras

AH-1J

Armament Configuration	20mm M197 Cannon	2.75-in M229 Rockets	7.62mm M18 Minigun	TOW Missiles	Fuel
Basic Combat (9,832 lb gross wt)	750 rds	14 rds	-	-	1600 lb
Medium Combat (10,000 lb gross wt)	750 rds	14 rds	2500 rds	-	1113 lb
Heavy Combat (10,000 lb gross wt)	155 rds	62 rds	-	-	395 lb

AH-1T

Armament Configuration	20mm M197 Cannon	2.75-in M229 Rockets	7.62mm M18 Minigun	TOW Missiles	Fuel
Basic Combat (12,321 lb gross wt)	750 rds	14 rds	-	-	2120 lb
Medium Combat (12,976 lb gross wt)	750 rds	14 rds	2500 rds	-	2120 lb
Heavy Combat (14,000 lb gross wt)	750 rds	62rds	-	-	1616 lb

Other armament that can be carried by the SeaCobras: M118 Smoke Grenade Dispenser, CBU-55 Fuel Air Explosive, MK45 Parachute Flare, MK115 Bomb, Hellfire Missile System, and SUU-44 Flare Dispenser.

AH-1T/TOW

Armament Configuration	20mm M197 Cannon	2.75-in M229 Rockets	7.62mm M18 Minigun	TOW Missiles	Fuel
Basic Combat (12,120 lb gross wt)	750 rds	-	-	4 rds	2120 lb
Medium Combat (12,456 lb gross wt)	750 rds	-	-	8 rds	2120lb
Heavy Combat (12,994 lb gross wt)	750 rds	14 rds	-	8 rds	2120 lb

* The LAU-68 normally dispensed 7 rockets while the LAU-61 and LAU-68 held 19 rockets.

AH-1J
U.S. Marine Corps

Armament

Legend:

M197 - 20MM cannon
M18 - 7.62 minigun pod
M118 - Smoke grenade dispenser
CBU-55 - Fuel air explosive
LAU-68 - 7 rockets
LAU-69 - 19 rockets
LAU-61 - 19 rockets
MK45 - Parachute Flare
MK115 - Bomb
HMMS - Hellfire modular missile system
SUU-44 - Flare dispenser

XM118	M18	M197	M18	XM118
CBU-55/B	CBU-55/B	M197	CBU-55/B	CBU-55/B
SUU-44	SUU-44	M197	SUU-44	SUU-44
MK115	LAU-68/A	M197	LAU-68/A	MK115
MK45	LAU-68B/A	M197	LAU-68B/A	MK45
LAU-69/A	LAU-69/A	M197	LAU-69/A	LAU-69/A
LAU-61/A	LAU-61/A	M197	LAU-61/A	LAU-61/A
LAU-68/A	LAU-68/A	M197	LAU-68/A	LAU-68/A
4 HMMS		M197		4 HMMS

171

AH-1T
U.S. Marine Corps

Armament

Legend:

M197   20MM cannon
LAU-68   7 rockets
M18   7.62m minigun pod

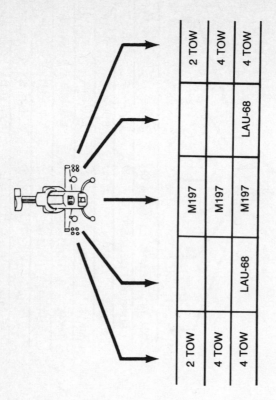

2 TOW		M197		2 TOW
4 TOW		M197	LAU-68	4 TOW
4 TOW	LAU-68	M197	LAU-68	4 TOW

Note:
SEE AH-1J FOR NON-TOW AH-1T CONFIGURATIONS

U.S. Air Force Hueys at a Glance

	UH-1F TH-1F UH-1P	HH-1H	UH-1N VH-1N
Model			
Missions	Missile Site Support Special Operations Training Medevac Cargo/ Personnel	Rescue Missle Site Support Medevac Cargo/ Personnel	Rescue VIP Transport Special Operations Medevac Cargo/ Personnel
Powerplant	T58-GE-3	T53-L-13B	T400-CP-400
No. of Engines	1	1	2
Total Horsepower	1272	1400	1800
Rotor			
Blade Length	48 ft	48 ft	48 ft
Blade Chord	21 in	21 in	23 in
Weights			
Max. Gross	9000 lb	9500 lb	10,500 lb
Empty	4496 lb	5430 lb	5958 lb
Internal Cargo	170 cu ft	220 cu ft	220 cu ft
External Load	4000 lb	4000 lb	4000 lb
Internal Fuel Capacity	245 gal	211 gal	200 gal
Performance			
Max. Cruise(1)	100 knts	125 knts	114 knts
Max. Range(2)	308 nm	248 nm	232 nm
Hover Ceiling(1)			
IGE	9900 ft	9800 ft	12400 ft
OGE	5100 ft	4500 ft(3)	5000 ft
Rate of Climb(1)	1080 fpm	1600 fpm	1660 fpm
Vertical R/C(1)	620 fpm	380 fpm(3)	340 fpm

Notes: (1) Sea Level at Maximum Gross Weight, except as noted
(2) Sea Level at Maximum Gross Weight with Standard Fuel
(3) Gross wt. = 9000 lb

Commercial Hueys at a Glance

	204B	205A-1	212 TWIN TWO-TWELVE	214B Biglifter	214ST SUPER TRANSPORT	412
First Delivery	1963	1967	1971	1975	1982	1981
Dimensions						
Fuselage Length	39.6 ft	40.7 ft	42.5 ft	44.1 ft	49.4 ft	42.4 ft
Overall Height	14.6 ft	14.6 ft	14.4 ft	15.0 ft	16.2 ft	15.1 ft
Rotor Blade Dia.	48 ft	48 ft	48.1 ft	50 ft	52 ft	46 ft
Rotor Blade Chord	21 in	21 in	23 in	33 in	33 in	14 in
Powerplant						
Manufacturer	Lycoming	Lycoming	P&W	Lycoming	GE	P&W
Designation	T53-9/11	T53-L-13B	PT6T-3B	T5508	CT7-2A	PT6T-3B
Total Horsepower	1100	1400	1800	2930	3250	1800
Number of Engines	1	1	2	1	2	2
Capacities						
Internal Cargo	140 cu ft	248 cu ft	248 cu ft	248 cu ft	381 cu ft	248 cu ft
External Load	4000 lb	5000 lb	5000 lb	8000 lb	8000 lb	5000 lb
Crew + Passengers	1 + 9	1 + 14	1 + 14	2 + 14	2 + 18	1 + 14
Standard Fuel	160 gal	220 gal	215 gal	-	435 gal	217 gal
Performance						
Max Gross Wt (int)	8500 lb	9500 lb	11,200	13,800 lb	17,500	11,600
Max Gross Wt (ext)	9500 lb	10,500 lb	11,200	16,00 lb	17,500	11,600
SL Max Cruise Speed	125 mph	138 mph	115 mph	160 mph	148 mph	140 mph
Range at SL	343 miles	303 miles	260 miles	285 miles	500 miles	248 miles
Hover Ceiling IGE	9600 ft	12,200 ft	11,000 ft	15,000 ft	6400 ft	9200 ft
OGE	4400 ft	6300 ft	-	10,500 ft	1000 ft	-
SL Rate of Climb	1060 fpm	1680 fpm	1420 fpm	2200 fpm	1780 fpm	1350 fpm
Vertical R/C at SL	780 fpm	1000 fpm	-	910 fpm	-	-

NOTE: Performance given for Maximum Gross Internal Loading Weights and Standard Fuel Load

Comparisons: UH-1H Versus UH-60A

	UH-1H	UH-60A
Main Rotor Diameter	48 ft	53.7 ft
Tail Rotor Diameter	8.5 ft	11 ft
Overall Length	44.9 ft	53.7 ft
Maximum Height	14.6 ft	16.8 ft
Total Engine Horsepower	1400	3120
Empty Weight	5210 lbs	10,900 lbs
Maximum Gross Weight	9500 lbs	20,250 lbs
Useful Load (internal)	4000 lbs	6,000 lbs
(external)	4000 lbs	8,000 lbs
Maximum SL Cruise Speed	110 kts	160 kts

AH-1G Versus AH-64A

	AH-1G	AH-64A
Main Rotor Diameter	44 ft	48 ft
Tail Rotor Diameter	8.5 ft	9.1 ft
Overall Length (Rotor Turning)	53 ft	58.1 ft
Overall Height	13.5 ft	15.2 ft
Fuselage Width	3 ft	4 ft
Total Engine Horsepower	1400	3388
Empty Weight	5816 lbs	10,600 lbs
Maximum Gross Weight	9500 lbs	20,700 lbs
Useful Mission Load	2812 lbs	6152 lbs
Maximum SL Cruise Speed	129 kts	160 kts

Index

176

SeaCobra use in, 88
USMC helicopters used in, 71

W

Westmoreland, William, 51
Wingate's Raiders, 2

X

XH-40 helicopter, 11, 12, 13, 14, 16, 141
XH-48A helicopter, 95
XP-59A jet aircraft, 4
XT53 Lycoming engine, 13

Y

YAG-1Q prototype helicopter, 67
YAH-1s prototype helicopters, 67, 144
YAH-63 advanced attack helicopter, 151, 154
YH-40 helicopter, 13, 14, 16
YUH-1B, 142
YUH-1D Huey prototypes, 41, 146

Z

Zuni rockets, 92

Edited by Steven H. Mesner

Other Bestsellers From TAB